Richard F. Speight, Jr.

Real Fruit

Receiving and Giving Jesus' Real Love

Real Fruit

Published by:
Intermedia Publishing, Inc.
P.O. Box 2825
Peoria, Arizona 85380
www.intermediapub.com

ISBN 978-1-937654-17-7

Printed in the United States of America

To my brother Dan,
You are His man of blazing love!

Richard T. Spangler

12/13/12

Psalm 27

Josh 5:13 ff....

Recommendations

"REAL FRUIT puts your spiritual journey on solid ground. Richard Speight weaves real life experiences with scriptural insights yielding life-changing applications. Enjoy the feast of fruit!"

Kenneth Young
Energy Efficiency Consultant
Columbus, Nebraska

"Richard Speight writes out of his dwelling place with his Heavenly Father with personal and practical insight. I found myself marveling, meditating, and rejoicing in REAL FRUIT!"

David Grandon
Pastor, Open Bible Church
Jefferson, Iowa

"With incredible insight on every page, Richard Speight takes us on a joyous stroll through the vineyard of the truly fruitful life the Holy Spirit so longs for us to have."

Caleb Plumb
Pastor, Encounter Christian Church
Cedar Rapids, Iowa

"Pastor Speight's memorable stories remind me just how much Jesus loved me even as I tried the 'plastic' fake things in life. Jesus is the real deal, so why would I stand in the way of the fruitful life He has for me?"

Dr. Michael Goad, D.C.
Sterling Bridge Place
Cedar Rapids, Iowa

"The journey awaiting you in these pages is not for the faint of heart. With surgical precision, REAL FRUIT cuts away things keeping us anemic and points us to a Great Doctor and a Great Cure."

Travis Kolder
Church Planter, C.R. House Church Network
Cedar Rapids, Iowa

"Arising from Richard's lived experience and prayerful discernment, REAL FRUIT leads you to tap into God's generous and bountiful larder. A must read for those hungry for real food for the journey."

Sister Nancy Hoffman
F.S.P.A., Prairiewoods Spirituality/Ecology Center
Hiawatha, Iowa

"Richard Speight is relentless in his pursuit of closer relationship with Jesus. This book is a true advancement into the kingdom of God."

Brice Ford, Men's Ministry Leader
River of Life Ministries
Cedar Rapids, Iowa

"Want real fruit in your Christian life? No matter what's going on around you, Christ wants you to manifest the fruit of the Holy Spirit. Richard Speight shows you how in REAL FRUIT—it's the real deal!"

John P. Kelly
Convening Apostle, ICA (International Coalition of Apostles);
Visionary Founder, LEAD (Leadership Education for Advancement and Development)
Ft. Worth, Texas

"Only open these pages if you want your understanding of God to explode. Richard Speight shares truths from our Lord that stretch us. For the first time you may say, 'I've got it. Now, I've got to go share it.'"

Glenn Shields
CEO, 21st Century Strategic Forums, L.L.C.
St. Louis, Missouri

"Richard is one of the voices Jesus is using in our generation to call us back to Kingdom living. In REAL FRUIT come closer to our Father, listen for His voice, and obey in the real fruit of the Spirit!"

Marty Boller
Vineyard Pastor and Pastoral Coach
Cedar Rapids, Iowa

"I'm blessed by the simplicity of Richard's real life stories, transparent honesty, and practical insights to grasp the depth of Jesus' real love. This is a must read for real followers of Christ."

Stephen Russell
Pastor, Jordan's Grove Church
Central City, Iowa

This book is dedicated in honor of my father,
Richard Forrestt Speight, Sr.
who taught me how to give and receive real love
as a husband and father.

Acknowledgments

I am grateful to many during the
writing of this book.

The Lord for His arms of love.

All the friends of Come Rest for
bountiful prayer, support, and bearing
real fruit with us.

David and Mary Grandon for
providing Come Away Cottage for our
writing getaways.

Our friends at Intermedia Publishing
Group for prompt, professional
assistance.

My in-laws; Arnold and Merilee,
my dad, and many family members
cheering us on.

My wonderful children; daughter
Emily for her caring expertise, and son
Daniel for his encouraging humor.

Finally, my beautiful Kimberly for
rigorous editing, patient counsel,
faithfulness, and true love!

Richard Speight
February 2012

Contents

Part 6: Kindness

Part 7: Goodness

Part 8: Faithfulness

Part 9: Gentleness

Part 10: Self-control

Part 11: The Adventure Ahead

INTRODUCTION

FEAST OR FAMINE

This is real love—not that we loved God, but that he loved us and sent his Son as a sacrifice to take away our sins... We love each other because he loved us first.

—1 John 4:10, 19

Think back over your last seventy-two hours. How many times has someone poured out lavish words and deeds of unconditional affirmation and kindness upon you? How many times have you poured out such no-strings-attached love upon others? This is not to take you on a guilt trip or to make you sad, but to invite you to a wonderful adventure! There is a famine of love in the world. There is a severe lack of God's no-strings-attached love received and given everywhere. The Lord is alerting you to this famine because He wants to help you end it!

People are starving for the real thing and feeding on poor substitutes. The world idolizes false love in many forms; sex, sentimentality, manipulation, flattery, good works, or reciprocal affection.

The Bible has the only true definition of real love. The real thing only comes from Jesus through those who are in a personal love relationship with Him.

Jesus wants to give you a truly fruitful life, to make you His child of real love. He wants you to make real changes so you can make a real difference in this love starved world.

And many false prophets...will deceive many people. Sin will be rampant... and the love of many will grow cold. Matthew 24:11-13

Jesus said the day would come where sin is rampant, many of His followers' hearts will grow cold, and many will be deceived by the evil one. The Lord doesn't want that for you, your loved ones, or even your enemies. You have been led to this book to prevent your heart from growing cold and to help you grow totally ablaze in His love!

You can't give real love without first receiving it. It's hard to receive real love if you don't understand what it is, and what it isn't. We can't bear real fruit if we are feeding on false fruit. The world is in a feeding frenzy of fear. People are settling for false fruit instead of the real thing. Like survivors of a shipwreck on a life raft, we can be tempted to slake our desperate thirst with seawater which only dehydrates us accelerating our demise. The famine of love will get worse in the days ahead for everyone who does not draw closer to Jesus.

I have told you all this so that you may have peace in me... take heart, because I have overcome the world. John 16:33

The Lord is neither worried nor threatened. He said these days would come. He wants you to take heart. He is not resting until He helps as many as possible come rest in Him. He is preparing the world for His return and sending out one last call from Matthew 11:28, "Come to Me all who are weary and heavy laden and I will give you rest." He alone offers rest from sin, rest from a cold heart, and rest from deception. Again, He alone offers real fruit in this famine of love.

But the Holy Spirit produces this kind of fruit in our lives: love, joy, peace, patience, kindness, goodness, faithfulness, gentleness, and self-control. Galatians 5:22-23

In all who truly yield to Jesus, the Holy Spirit will yield these nine real fruit to be life saving nourishment for others. In this book you will find Scriptures, simple truths, and stories to help you identify false fruit so you can feast on and bear His real fruit.

The reflection/discussion guide in the back of the book can help you enter into a deeper conversation with the Lord. Use the guide as you read chapter by chapter or for review after you finish. Consider gathering a group of your friends for discussion of the book, testimonies, encouragement, and prayer. Enjoy!

Jesus said He will return like a thief in the night when He is least expected. It's not yet too late for each of us to begin afresh with Him. No matter how unfruitful one's life may have been—we can still become all He wants us to be!

Jesus wants to grow you bursting with His love! The moment you begin to truly live for Him, He promises to make your life fruitful beyond your wildest dreams.

You will be like a well-watered garden, like an ever-flowing spring. Isaiah 58:11

Stop feeding on "plastic" fruit and start feasting on the real thing. Become like an overflowing garden of real love, real fruit.

Come grow. Come flow. Come end the famine of love.

INVITATION

Chapter 1

Your Unguarded Heart

Let the children come to me. Don't stop them! ...I tell you the truth, anyone who doesn't receive the Kingdom of God like a child will never enter it.

—Luke 18:16-17

I teach a class at our church called "Resting in Jesus as a Lifestyle." One day a man who had been in class for over a year came to me with a question. He was a retired U.S. Navy Chief Petty Officer and a man of few words. He asked a truly exposing question, "I hear what you say about letting Jesus love you and lead you… but how does one begin?" He was opening up for help from the teacher who supposedly knew the answer!

Have you ever given someone a "pretty good" answer? I said, "Well, the first thing you do is start honestly talking to the Lord. You ask Him for help. You begin a conversation. It's called prayer."

That seemed to help him for the moment, but I felt a nagging dissatisfaction. Three days later while praying and writing in my journal, I realized that before a person can begin talking with God they must first let down their guard to Him.

Suddenly I saw a picture in my mind of the whole world, believers and not-yet-believers, walking around on guard toward the Lord. It's so easy in this fearful world to almost unconsciously adopt a self-protective stance toward everyone, including Jesus! As the picture in my mind unfolded I saw everyone with shoulders hunched carrying lots of baggage they could use to build a wall at a moment's notice. I saw that people were not so much talking *to* God as just saying prayers. People can't really talk *with* God until they let down their guard, until they truly open themselves up to Him like a child.

The Lord knows you have baggage from traveling through this life. Your walls do not discourage Him. He will wait with open arms of love as long as it takes for you to trust Him just enough.

I remember skinning my knee as a child. I instinctively held my hand on the wound and would not let my mother look. She reassured me giving me time to settle down and remember it was *her* kneeling in front of me. I could trust *her. She* knew my "owie" could not begin to heal until I trusted *her* just enough to take my hand off so she could look, cleanse, and kiss it. *Jesus* loves you more than you know. He knows your wounds and waits for you with reassuring, cleansing, healing love.

You are very young to the Lord. You are older than you have ever been—but you are very, very young to Him. So why not act like it? What have you got to lose except your wounds, your weariness, and your walls?

Above all else, guard your heart, for it is the wellspring of life. Proverbs 4:23 NIV

He's not asking you to be reckless. He wants you to guard your heart at all times from evil because He made it to be the place from which His spirit wells up. However, his Spirit doesn't well up until you let down your guard to Him.

I have come as a light to shine in this dark world, so that all who put their trust in me will no longer remain in the dark. John 12:46

Stay here a moment with Him. Would you take your hand off the wound? What is it that you dare not expose to Him? What pain, what fear, what shame? He already knows. He already loves. He is "all-ready" exposing His fiery heart of love to you. Are you ready enough?

Darkness does not come in various shades. The moment a match is lit in a dark room, darkness leaves by definition. The moment you begin to lift your hand from the wound His healing fountain of light flows.

No more darkness, no more walls… let down your guard to this One. He never guards His heart from you.

Let's pray:

Lord Jesus, I turn to you face to face and let down my guard. Help me learn to always guard my heart from evil and never guard my heart from YOU! I'm looking forward to all You will do with me and through me. Amen.

Chapter 2

Silos and Sand Dunes

Have faith in me, and you will have life-giving water flowing from deep inside you, just as the Scriptures say.

—John 7:37 Contemporary English Version

After I realized the importance of letting down our guard to the Lord, a powerful picture came to mind. Christians around the world looked like shut up silos full of grain in a Saharan landscape. On any given day most people receive no loving words, no loving touch. There is a famine of love in the land, yet the Lord is our storehouse within.

Then came an explosive sequence. I saw each follower of Jesus choosing to *let down their guard* to Jesus, opening to *receive* His love. I saw the silo doors opening and grain spilling out. This moment by moment choice *released* the overflow of real love to others. When each let their guard down to His love *for them*, the silos were opened and released His nourishing love *for everyone else* around them. His very presence was welling up from within each believer and pouring into love starved lives.

The flow of real love is released from us the moment we receive it. *Receiving is releasing!* The overflow of real love into others' lives only comes from letting Jesus love us.

We love, because He first loved us. 1 John 4 NASB

There is a famine of love in the world because there is a famine of love in Christians. We can't give what we aren't first receiving. We have vastly underestimated real love which is the real fruit of the Spirit. Some think of the fruit of the Spirit as Christlike character traits. Some think of the fruit of the Spirit as the words and actions of Christians. While those are "pretty good" explanations, there is so much more!

Since God *is* love, then the Holy Spirit is the person who makes the love of the Father and the Son *real* on earth through His fruit growing and flowing *out* of the lives of true believers.

But the Holy Spirit produces this kind of fruit in our lives: love, joy, peace, patience, kindness, goodness, faithfulness, gentleness, and self-control. There is no law against these things! Galatians 5:22-23

Notice that "love" is the first fruit on the list. The Holy Spirit has a purpose for the sequence of words in Scripture. He placed "love" first on the list because God *is* love. Therefore, the Holy Spirit only births and grows LOVE. The other fruit on the list are eight related unique expressions of real love. When we trust Jesus by letting down our guard to Him the Holy Spirit is the living water who flows out of us! The fruit of the Spirit is real live love growing and flowing out of you in *three* ways—your Spirit led words; your Spirit led actions; and the untamed presence of the Spirit *Himself.*

Take the phrase simply for what it says—"fruit of the Spirit." Fruit grows outward from within a plant. As you yield control of your life to Jesus, the Holy Spirit *grows* real love from within you *outward* into all your relationships and circumstances. In the process you become Christlike.

We complain about this unloving world while we are filled to bursting with the Solution. When we trust Jesus to be our provider and protector, his perfect love wells up within us to overflowing, casts out all fear, and we release all the real nourishing fruit of the Spirit.

How often in the last three days have you stopped to let down your guard to Jesus, talk to Him, listen to Him, read His word, sing to Him, repent to Him, or let go of burdens and grudges to Him? If you are presently a believer in Jesus, search your heart. How are you shutting yourself off from Jesus? What changes does He want you to make to receive and release His love?

If you are presently a non-believer you may be reading this because you want to know if Jesus is real or not. That's fair. You may have been repelled in the past because some Christian let you down. That's understandable. Yet, Jesus has never let you down. Why hold it against Him?

You may be presently attracted to Jesus because one of His followers is letting down their guard to Jesus and to you. That's how Jesus works!

Let down your guard to Jesus and experience the release of His endless wellspring of love *for* you and *through* you. Aren't you tired of the desert?

Chapter 3
A Contest of Wills

Is this not the fast that I have chosen: To loose the bonds of wickedness, To undo the heavy burdens, To let the oppressed go free, And that you break every yoke?

—Isaiah 58:6 New King James Version

Famine is a prolonged lack of necessary food placing the yoke of starvation upon an entire population. Though drought and insects are contributors, a principal cause is human choice—greed and mismanaged food, water, soil, and crop diversity.

There is a famine of love because we who claim the Lord won't do things His way. We won't really let Him love us and lead us. We often bluff when we claim to be His followers. Real believers must become real love receivers who are becoming real love givers. So goes the Kingdom. If you won't yield to the Lord, He won't yield His fruit through you. The stakes are too high as too many people are bound by wickedness.

In Isaiah 58 the Lord offers His true fast—true freedom from all forms of oppression. Isaiah 58 is fulfilled in Jesus who offers every person today an exchange: His Yoke of rest for the fearful yoke of the devil. Jesus "fasted" from his own well being by suffering unto death on the cross to break the yoke of sin and death over all humanity. Ever since He was raised from the dead, anyone who calls on His name with real trust will be saved. The Holy Spirit is on the move to break as many yokes and save as many people as possible before Jesus' returns. Will we move with Him?

Many years ago, Kim and I were visiting her sister's family. We were conversing at the kitchen table after lunch while her delightfully precocious child ate his chocolate dessert in his high chair. When he finished he said fairly politely, "More chockit Mama." She said, "No son, you've had enough." Not well received.

In a few moments he intoned more intently, "More chockit, Mama!" To which she replied firmly, "No." Auntie and Uncle now had to purse our lips to stifle grins. We felt a mix of emotions. He was so cute in his insistence, yet gravely in way over his head. He had failed to assess his mother's resolve.

Our conversation continued. We saw it coming but knew we could only sit by as he traversed the slippery slope. Suddenly nephew pounded both fists on his tray and screamed, "MORE CHOCKIT!!!" Instantly, his mother slammed her hand down on the table creating a resounding echo. "Mr. Chockit" sat up in wide eyed startled shock. She declared quietly and deliberately, "That is enough! Do you hear me?" He nodded silently and we heard not another peep, as he faced the consequences of his actions by sitting in the corner facing the wall. Her passionate plain talk and correction steered her beloved son away from the temptation of "spoiled bratdom."

It is so fortunate the Lord loves you and me the same way. He paid the full price for your sin and sends the Holy Spirit to seek you through the real love of other Christians. As you receive

Him as your Lord and Savior He adopts you as His own child. There is nothing required of you to be saved except to receive the gift of Jesus. What a deal!

However, after you become born again, He doesn't automatically grow you into a wonderful loving person. You must learn from Him to cooperate as a trusting obedient child. No fruit of the Spirit will grow in your life unless you let the Lord lead you. There is a lack of love in the world because too many of us are pounding our fists in our high chairs. We petulantly expect more *dessert* instead of bearing His fruit in the desert.

Unless you tap into His deep wellsprings, the Lord will not make your life a bountiful garden of produce for your love starved friends, family, and enemies. Yet, the Lord makes an amazing offer to you in Isaiah.

The LORD will guide you continually, giving you water when you are dry and restoring your strength. You will be like a well-watered garden, like an ever-flowing spring. Isaiah 58:11

If you will live for Him, He will make your life like a well-watered garden, like an ever flowing spring. This promise is made in the midst of some very passionate plain talk from the Lord.

In Isaiah's time people were performing self-centered religious rituals, yet were disappointed in God because He was not blessing them. They were acting like spoiled brats.

So the Lord laid it on the line through Isaiah. The Lord saw the people's penance and fasting as a big show. He was not impressed and would not bless them nor answer their prayers. They were acting religious to get benefits for themselves; not to honor Him and make sacrifices to help others. Plain and simple, they were not living for Him.

They were not really connecting with Him so there was no connection between their ritual and their relationships. They were not walking their talk. They weren't even talking the talk! In fact they would say "I'm sorry" to the Lord with the same mouth they were using to gossip, lie, and quarrel.

You can follow along in your Bible in Isaiah 58. The plain talk continues. If they really want Him to respond to their fasting and prayers then they would hunger after Him in loosening, untying, and breaking heavy yokes weighing people down. They were not sharing their own possessions with the hungry and homeless. They were hiding from their own relatives in need. They were always trying to squeeze more out of their workers instead of lightening their loads. If they really wanted the Lord to be their delight, then give Him one Sabbath day a week for rest from labor to enjoy Him and Him alone.

Isaiah 58 is the resounding echo through the ages of the Lord passionately calling the bluff of every person who is more into religion *about* Him rather than in real relationship *with* Him on a daily basis.

The same is true today. We can be churchgoers rich in religion but poor in real love. Going to church doesn't necessarily mean you are going to the Lord. Going to church really helps if your one desire is the Lord. The fruitful church is real adopted children of God passionately ablaze with real demonstrated love for Him *and* for people. It's serious business. It's a question of control, a contest of wills.

His resolve is much deeper than ours. That's a good thing because your own resolve will only get you so far before you tire of living for God and others. We all desperately need the constant help of the Holy Spirit.

Most would agree that everything the Lord says in Isaiah 58 is good stuff. But we really don't want to pay the price—dying to self, surrendering control. There is something in every human that does not want to be told what to do. It's called our sin nature. When we let our sin nature control us the results are ugly. But when we let the Holy Spirit control us the results are a beautiful well-watered garden. For the next few moments let the Lord speak a little more plain talk as the following words sink in like rain on thirsty ground.

So I say, let the Holy Spirit guide your lives. Then you won't be doing what your sinful nature craves. The sinful nature wants to do evil, which is just the opposite of what the Spirit wants. And the Spirit gives us desires that are the opposite of what the sinful nature desires. These two forces are constantly fighting each other, so you are not free to carry out your good intentions.

When you follow the desires of your sinful nature, the results are very clear: sexual immorality, impurity, lustful pleasures, idolatry, sorcery, hostility, quarreling, jealousy, outbursts of anger, selfish ambition, dissension, division, envy, drunkenness, wild parties, and other sins like these. Let me tell you again, as I have before, that anyone living that sort of life will not inherit the Kingdom of God. But the Holy Spirit produces this kind of fruit in our lives: love, joy, peace, patience, kindness, goodness, faithfulness, gentleness, and self-control. There is no law against these things! Those who belong to Christ Jesus have nailed the passions and desires of their sinful nature to his cross and crucified them there. Since we are living by the Spirit, let us follow the Spirit's leading in every part of our lives. Galatians 5:16-26

His plain talk is offering you a clear choice. It's the only contest of wills in the whole world where the loser wins. Will you?

Chapter 4

Well-Watered

Now there was a famine in the land... He moved away from there and dug another well, and they did not quarrel over it; so he named it Rehoboth, for he said, "At last the LORD has made room for us, and we will be fruitful in the land."

—Genesis 26:1-22 NASB

In a famine, Isaac dug three new wells. Locals argued over the first so Isaac named it "Argument." Locals opposed him for the second so he named it "Opposition." But at the third well, the locals neither argued nor opposed. He named the well *Rehoboth* meaning "room enough" for his family to be fruitful. This story symbolizes changes the Holy Spirit wants for you. If you stop quarreling and stop opposing His Word, He can lead you toward your best self. It's as if the Lord has a shovel in His hand and is inviting you to join Him in digging out every last bit of willful rebellion and quarreling in your daily life. Your will can become His well.

You will be like a well-watered garden, like an ever-flowing spring. Isaiah 58:11

The phrase "well-watered" does not mean expertly watered. You cannot expertly water and manicure the garden of your life.

Your life is not meant to look like a golf course. There are too many "traps" in that image! You cannot grow yourself. That's the way the world thinks and the lie the devil wants you to believe.

The phrase "well-watered" means He is the wellspring feeding you. The Lord spoke this through Isaiah to people who knew the life-or-death meaning of wellsprings in a desert. Your life is meant to be an oasis of His real fruit. An oasis has limited expansion in desert landscape depending upon depth and force of its spring. An aerial view of the Sahara would reveal sand dotted by few oases. But with the Holy Spirit as wellspring, our lives can become ever-expanding oases which eventually consume the desert!

I have come that they may have life, and that they may have it more abundantly. John 10:10 NKJV

The word "abundant" means lush overflowing life. When your well is clear of argument and rebellion there is no limit to how fruitful you can be! Rebellion means your will against His will, your words and actions against His Word. Quarreling is never placed in a positive light in the Bible. Therefore you rebel against Him every time you take the bait to quarrel. Quarreling requires two insecure people lashing out to damage, defeat, or manipulate each other.

They must not slander anyone and must avoid quarreling. Instead, they should be gentle and show true humility to everyone. Titus 3:2

What good is fasting when you keep on fighting and quarreling? This kind of fasting will never get you anywhere with me. Isaiah 58:4

Quarrelsome thinking is like locusts hastening famine. You can try to feel more secure by labeling people. Quarreling requires you to rebel against God's word by setting yourself against another's personhood. If you can label and dehumanize someone it's easier for you to control them. We have all stumbled in this. There is only One in the world who is lovingly right all of the time. The rest of us on any given day are either filling our wells in rebellion or emptying ourselves toward His overflowing presence.

We even try to pigeonhole God. There is not an Old Testament God and a New Testament God. The Father, Son, and Holy Spirit have always been and will always be. The Lord always loves you and always hates your sin. He gives you freedom to receive or reject His love. That's why He says "Come to Me." You choose to accept His invitation. If you won't He seeks you until you die.

Real love never gives up. But some people won't give themselves up to the Lord. Real love is freely chosen. It is not love to mind my own business if you are destroying yourself. It is love to offer you truth, invite you to change, and offer to help you. It is not love to give up on you. It is love to never quit lifting you up to God in prayer. It is impossible to force you to receive and give real love. Love cannot be coerced. But it will hurt me to see you hurting yourself. The Lord hurts even more for you.

He hates your sin because you deprive yourself and others of love. The more you fill your well with gunk the less the Holy Spirit will flow through you, the more people are deprived of love through you, the more people around you will be tempted to choose false love, the more likely they will not come to Jesus, the more likely they go to hell when they die. It's that painfully true. He hates that. Let this be the one thing you truly hate—people receiving no real love and ending up in hell separated from God forever. Jesus is a true friend of sinners, but He is an enemy of sin. He wants no person to go to hell. That's why He took all our sins upon Himself.

For even the Son of Man came not to be served but to serve others and to give his life as a ransom for many. Mark 10:45

If you want to be a real friend to sinners, you must become an enemy of sin, particularly your own. Dig the logs out of the well!

How can you think of saying, 'Friend, let me help you get rid of that speck in your eye,' when you can't see past the log in your own eye? ...Hypocrite! First get rid of the log in your own eye; then you will see well enough to deal with the speck in your friend's eye." Luke 6:42

The Lord humorously refers to your sin as a "log" because you need His help to dig it out. Once you do, He will lead you to help others with their well digging. Come rest from running your life or anyone else. Only a heart resting secure in Jesus' arms will not argue with another soul. Your future can overflow with real fruit consuming the desert!

Dig well.

The LORD will comfort Israel again and have pity on her ruins. Her desert will blossom like Eden, her barren wilderness like the garden of the LORD. Joy and gladness will be found there. Songs of thanksgiving will fill the air. Isaiah 51:3

Let's pray:

Jesus ebb and Jesus flow.
May Your love rise within my soul.
Jesus ebb and Jesus flow.
Let Your love rise within my soul.
Amen.

LOVE

Real Love:
Unconditional Sacrifice

Plastic Love:
Mutual Self-interest

Chapter 5

Accept No Substitutes

We do this by keeping our eyes on Jesus, the champion who initiates and perfects our faith. Because of the joy awaiting him, he endured the cross, disregarding its shame. Now he is seated in the place of honor beside God's throne.

—Hebrews 12:2

Sandy Koufax was my childhood hero. He was #32, the left-handed flame throwing pitcher for the Los Angeles Dodgers. Sandy mowed down the mighty New York Yankees in the 1963 World Series. I dreamed of becoming the star left-hander, #32, of the Dodgers someday. As it turned out, there were two minor details I could not overcome—I was right-handed and I didn't have much talent!

In April of 1964 hope was springing anew as I began my weekly pilgrimage to Hannan's corner grocery store to begin building my collection of Major League trading cards for the new season. In those days, you would trade your nickel for a five-card package including one large stick of rather tasteless bubble gum. But you weren't buying the package for the gum. When I wanted the real thing in bubble gum in those days I bought

"Bazooka Joe." The little comic about "Joe" was okay but the gum was the genuine article with lasting taste and bubbles!

My quest, of course, was not gum but to acquire all the Dodgers and to find the rare Koufax card, the "holy grail" that year amongst pre-teen boys in America. Trading card marketers always placed the superstars few and far between all the rookies and utility outfielders to motivate continual purchases. In those days cards were released piecemeal and one couldn't buy the whole league collection or a team en masse like today. As a kid in a blue collar neighborhood of Council Bluffs, Iowa, I got one nickel a week with occasional permission from my parents to spend a whole quarter on five packs! The quest continued deep into summer. I was delighted with Maury Wills, Don Drysdale, Johnny Roseborough, and Willie Davis… but still no #32!

Finally, one afternoon I bought my usual single pack, but walked all the way home before I opened it. There he was, Sandy smiling at me! His card that year was an up close shot in which his face filled the whole frame! I was so happy; I couldn't wait to tell my best friend next door. He was a Yankee fan and wasn't as happy as I at the acquisition. Still he, and every other kid in the neighborhood, had respect for the card. None of us knew anyone who had it. The scarcity of the Koufax card was its value to all the non-Koufax fans. But to me, the card was precious because Koufax was my favorite.

The next day it began. My best friend began trade offers. Right off the bat he offered me his Mickey Mantle card for my Koufax. The others in the neighborhood, all one or two years older than me, said it was a great deal. After all, they said, Mantle had been great for so many more years than Koufax. At that point it was not hard to resist. No way!

However, my friend continued to “sweeten the pot” adding other Yankee stars to his offer. This seemingly represented his sacrifice since he was offering so many cards. I continued to resist, noting that he already had duplicates of everything he was offering me. Finally, my friend received rookie star Joe Pepitone (a card he did not have) and added him immediately to Mantle, Tresh, Richardson, Berra, Boyer, Howard, and Maris. I began to weaken spurred on by other kids in the neighborhood saying what an amazing deal it was.

Suddenly, I yielded to greed and I took the bait impulsively making the trade. I remember the disgust I immediately felt that only grew with the taunting of my friends. As the younger kid, I had not realized the competition my Koufax card had engendered. It was a hard lesson learned. As I emerged from the fog of covetousness I realized that I now owned cards of all the Yankee stars Sandy Koufax had struck out! They were worthless to me and Sandy was gone.

I was angry at my friends and myself. I felt stupid and ashamed. For a few days I didn’t want to even think about baseball cards. Then I decided to resume my visits to Hannan’s. I bought one package, stared at it a moment, then slowly unwrapped it. When I got to the third card, there he was, smiling Sandy! It was unbelievable… yet, not really. Since that day, I have always believed the Lord gave me that card after I had learned my lesson. Grace upon grace. I’m not saying I never again gave into temptation or greed. But often when I have stumbled, repented, learned, and felt the Lord’s radical generosity of forgiveness and cleansing, He has taken me back to the summer of ’64.

It’s an ongoing ever deepening lesson in the school of real love. Sandy’s card was valuable to me, not because of its rarity, but because Sandy, the person, was my favorite. When I lost sight of the person I valued, I put my eyes on the things I might acquire. So goes greed.

But, Jesus is so good.

Again, the kingdom of heaven is like a merchant seeking beautiful pearls, who, when he had found one pearl of great price, went and sold all that he had and bought it. Matthew 13:45-46 NKJV

To Him we are each the pearl of great price, each one His favorite! He is such love, so good, so radically generous that He is the only person who can have seven and a half billion favorites at one time!

You are the pearl of great price. You are infinitely valuable to the Lord because you are His favorite. You are loved more than you know. He acted on that love by taking the penalty for your sin, your lust, your greed, your lies, your hate upon Himself. If you place your trust in Him asking Him to be the Lord of your life, this is the promise He makes, "I give them eternal life, and no one will be able to snatch them from my hand."

You are the real thing to Him. You are His focus. Jesus would never trade you for anything. Living with *you forever* was the "joy awaiting Him." You are why He endured the cross. Therefore, rest from the lower desires within you and settle for nothing less than Him. He is the only source of real love, real joy, real peace, real patience, real kindness, real faithfulness, real goodness, real gentleness, and real self-control.

In the Bible, there was a man named Esau who gave into his hunger and traded away his precious birthright blessing for a bowl of soup.

Jesus is the rare One. There is no one else who comes close. Accept no substitutes. Settle for nothing less than the One who was your Substitute on the Cross. Real love comes only from Him to this love starved world.

When Jesus had all the forces of hell tempting Him to take his eyes off you, he stayed the course and gave His life as a ransom for you, and me, and all humanity! Anyone who calls out to Him will be saved.

Sandy Koufax, baseball champion of my childhood, gave me great happiness which I was nonetheless willing to trade away for lesser things. That kind of happiness is nothing next to the real joy found in my true Champion's Arms.

Accept no substitute.

Chapter 6

Freely and Lightly

For where your treasure is, there will your heart be also.

—Matthew 6:21 KJV

I am a recovering sentimentalist. I used to have great difficulty letting go of things to which I had become emotionally attached. On my first day of college I went to the bookstore and bought a navy blue t-shirt with "Nebraska" printed across the chest. I wore it regularly for years and I finally placed it threadbare on the upper shelf "pantheon" of my closet.

After I married I would still wear it on special occasions. Kim had a hard time seeing anything "special" about the rag shirt. As a newlywed, she would just chuckle and shake her head. Soon, however, she saw I could be a packrat who could fill our house like Fibber McGee's closet of old radio show days!

One day I wore the rag shirt in front of company. Kim calmly notified me that if I wanted to keep the shirt in a drawer that was fine but if I wore it again she would simply come tear it off of me. She had that look in her eye I would call "playful ferocity."

Later, I forgot her promise and walked into the kitchen one morning wearing the shirt. Kim headed straight for me in front of the kids. I saw that look in her eye as she saw me begin to laugh. She promptly tore the shirt off my back and ripped it into several pieces. I don't know how long the four of us laughed but it was long and loud.

It was a moment of delightful freedom for me. In those days I would have said I really loved that shirt! But shirts aren't for loving, they are for wearing! I can now look back and see I was sentimentally attached to that shirt, big time! Sentimental attachment is a false expression of love.

I had not yet learned the difference between sentimental attachment and grateful memories. It's a question of misplaced treasure. In my love relationship with God I can look back and thank Him for good times and savor the memories as gifts from Him. Sentimental attachment focuses on things. Real love focuses on the Maker of all things.

Keepsakes are not bad in and of themselves except when our heart is attached to them. Kim makes amazing scrapbooks that help our family look back with gratitude to God for the precious gift of people and life experiences. I have a few things which engender grateful memories, but we also have an uncluttered, peaceful house! Kim has taught me that cherishing memories is different than accumulating the clutter of sentimental attachments.

God built you to love Him and people unconditionally, no strings *attached.* Unfortunately, when you do not make your relationship with Him your one true treasure, then you start "treasuring" people, other living creatures, or things. People are for loving, not latching. Things are for creative use or recreational play.

Real loving intimacy with the Him is not about attachment, but rather embrace. Your hands have to be empty to be free to embrace the Lord, to be free to walk with Him, to be free to reach out to love others.

Are you tired? Worn out? Burned out on religion? Come to me. Get away with me and you'll recover your life. I'll show you how to take a real rest. Walk with me and work with me—watch how I do it. Learn the unforced rhythms of grace. I won't lay anything heavy or ill-fitting on you. Keep company with me and you'll learn to live freely and lightly. Matthew 11:28-30 The Message

He wants you to live freely and lightly, without attachments, in constant companionship with Him. He is a real person who loves you, not a distant deity. "Deity" includes the word "it." He is not a thing to which you attach. He is not a distant higher power, a monster, a slot machine, a security blanket, nor a figment of the imagination. He is not "ultimate reality" with which you merge into a cosmic collective and lose your personal identity.

He is the person who made you, died for you, and lives for you. He hopes with all His heart you will love him back with all yours.

He wants you to make companionship with Him, your only real treasure. Then you will be free to fruitfully enjoy and use the things of life He has given you. Leave all other attachments and rest securely in His arms. He wants you to give Him continual permission to lead you on His mission. Trust He knows best. He wants you to get personal with Him. He wants you to get real. He wants to make you into the *real* you that He longs for you to be.

There is a famine of love because people treat God like a thing which leads to treating things like people and people like things.

I have a dear pastor friend named Steve Russell. He has been such an encouragement to me and countless others. He says, "Whatever you grip will grip you." Ponder that a moment. Whatever you treasure will have hold of you. Be very selective. Are you weary and heavy laden about anything right now? Are there unhealthy entanglements with relationships, work, finances, or anything else?

Real love is powerfully emotional. God *so* loved the world that He gave His only Son! However, real love is much more than emotion. Real love includes healthy emotional intimacy not misguided emotional attachment.

Love famine comes when you latch onto people and things *led around by the nose* by emotion to use people like things.

Love's Fruit comes when you embrace only Jesus and are *led around by the Spirit* to care for people and use things with care.

What, or Who, are you gripping? Do you want to live freely and lightly?

Chapter 7

Rest-oration

I am the good shepherd; the good shepherd lays down His life for the sheep. He who is a hired hand, and not a shepherd, who is not the owner of the sheep, sees the wolf coming, and leaves the sheep and flees, and the wolf snatches them and scatters them...

—John 10:11-12 NASB

My dad is a tenderhearted man who loved my mother faithfully for almost fifty-three years before she went to be with the Lord. I found childhood security in parents who treated one another as a gift from the Lord. They knew Jesus would never forsake them; therefore they would never forsake each other. There was a clear sense of "ownership" in our family. We belonged to Jesus. Through thick and thin, we knew Jesus would never give up on us, so we would not give up on each other. It's just the way it was. Thanks, Dad!

My dad is very responsible. If he owns something, he takes care of it. He sees to it that his modest home of fifty years is immaculate and sound. His 1994 Honda sedan is still in better shape than most late model cars.

If you had the choice between buying a three-year-old used car from a rental fleet and buying the same model with the same mileage from someone like my dad, which would you choose? No contest, right? With some exceptions, renters tend to abuse property while owners tend to preserve and improve their property. Ownership matters.

Have you ever said to a house guest, "Please come in and make yourself at home"? What would happen if you went to the kitchen and returned to find your houseguest had taken your pictures off the wall, drug your old comfortable furniture and plasma TV outside to the dumpster, and had begun tearing off old sheet rock?

I could hear myself yelling, "What do you think you're doing?" The guest might answer, "You told me to make myself at home." I might answer, "Well, yes, that's what I said but that's not what I meant. So sit down, shut up, and don't touch a thing! This is *my* house!"

If you ask Jesus to truly come into your life to be your Lord, He will! However, He doesn't come in as a guest or a renter. He comes to take ownership for a total makeover to help you become like Him.

Who is the owner of your life? Have you relinquished control of the house to Jesus? Or are you giving Him the equivalent of "sit down and shut up!"?

There is a famine of real love because there is a worldly kind of "ownership" in the "house" or family of Christ. We pastors can often think of church members as "*my* people." Church members can often think of church leaders as "*my* preacher" and the congregation as "*my* church." We don't own each other. When we even begin to think or act as if we have a right or claim to another person then we are on the slippery slope of manipulation.

What passes off for love is really what the world prizes as "mutual self-interest." "Scratch my back and I'll scratch yours" is the best the world has to offer and too often we settle for this plastic fruit.

God paid a high price for you, so don't be enslaved by the world. 1 Corinthians 7:23

The Lord is the only person in the world who can own you and not treat you as a slave. Instead He will cherish and prosper you as His beloved child with grace upon grace.

So we praise God for the glorious grace he has poured out on us who belong to his dear Son. He is so rich in kindness and grace that he purchased our freedom with the blood of his Son and forgave our sins. He has showered his kindness on us, along with all wisdom and understanding. Ephesians 1:6-8

Only One has bought us at a great price by suffering and dying for us. The Good Shepherd laid down His life to pay the ransom for our souls. He bought us to set us free in the hope we would let Him lead us in a real love relationship. That's His kind of ownership!

Real spiritual authority to watch over others has nothing to do with academic training, social skills, or even spiritual gifts. Real authority to lead is found in one's grateful willingness to lay one's life down for the sheep. Real authority is rooted in real love.

Many people answer the Lord's call to leading others with a genuine desire to love the Lord and love people. Unfortunately, many let their love grow cold in pursuit of spiritual leadership as a "career path." Jesus calls it being a "hireling."

Too many find their identity as "professional clergy" rather than as beloved children of God given the privilege of serving as Jesus served. Too many church members buy into this suffocation by either treating pastors as their employees or deferring to the pastors as if they are superiors. Either way there is little real fruit after tremendous expense of effort and money. Pastors can feel increasingly isolated and trapped in an impossible task and members can feel increasingly used, ignored, or bored.

The Lord understands all this and is moving these days to call us back to Him as our First Love. All believers are equals with unique callings in *His* Church.

He knows this oppressive professionalism has nothing to do with whether a pastor is paid a salary or not. It's all about motivation. A "hireling" church leader does it *for* money or *for* esteem and influence; His true shepherds do it *for* Him.

There will be no true "rest-oration" until the Lord's people rest from oration! His shepherds are filling the air with words out of their own anxiety and emptiness. His shepherds must let their words be few and let their words be His. His people also must rest from oration. They need to stop talking about His shepherds. His people and His shepherds often do not really love one another as brothers and sisters of His unconditional love. They often care for each other only to the extent they live up to each others' expectations. They often do not bear His fruit for they are snared in their fear of man. So continues the famine of love.

But He desires to bring real restoration in the fire of His love. He seeks to burn away your fear *of* man and replace it with His love *for* man!"

How about you? Are there strings attached to the positive actions you have toward other believers or leaders. Are your feelings and actions dependent upon how they treat you? Jesus says that's not real love.

If you love only those who love you, why should you get credit for that? Even sinners love those who love them! "Love your enemies! Do good to them. Lend to them without expecting to be repaid. Then your reward from heaven will be very great, and you will truly be acting as children of the Most High, for he is kind to those who are unthankful and wicked. You must be compassionate, just as your Father is compassionate. Luke 6:32, 35-36

It's awesome that the Lord's compassion is not dependent upon our actions toward Him! Your feelings and actions toward people must depend upon what Jesus has done for you, not what people have done for you. Real compassion is your loving desire *and* action on behalf of people regardless of their behavior. Famine of love comes when you do not give the real Owner his due.

I have a saying around our ministry, "We're stuck with each other!" I say it often to help us remember the Lord has made us adoptive family in His blood. Our Heavenly Father does not give up on us. We may stumble and hurt each other but we will not give up on each other!

After all, if you love Jesus and I love Jesus that means He loved us both first and that means we are family—stuck with each other for eternity—and that is a very good thing!

Most important of all, continue to show deep love for each other, for love covers a multitude of sins. 1 Peter 4:8

Ultimately, if the Lord is all we need we are free to love each other deep beneath the surface of our stumbling and bumbling—true unconditional love that covers the multitude of family squabbles.

That's when things really get exciting. The more not-yet saved people see Jesus' kinfolk truly loving each other the more they will see Him and come to Him. One of the most truly evangelistic things you can do is let Jesus lead you to unconditionally love your fellow believers. That's when the ever flowing spring of His presence erupts from you and starts splashing all around you—and your not-yet saved friends and relatives want in!

Most people want the Jesus who shines through unconditional love given and received. They just don't want a Church that acts any different than the "strings attached" world they encounter every day.

What sorrow awaits the leaders of my people...for they have destroyed and scattered the very ones they were expected to care for," says the LORD. But I will gather together the remnant of my flock... I will bring them back to their own sheepfold, and they will be fruitful and increase in number. Then I will appoint responsible shepherds who will care for them, and they will never be afraid again. Not a single one will be lost or missing... "For the time is coming...when I will raise up a righteous descendant from King David's line.... And this will be his name: 'The LORD Is Our Righteousness.' Jeremiah 23:1, 3-6

The Lord once spoke through a man named Jeremiah. He said there would come a day when He would shepherd people directly through a son of David who would be known as "The Lord our Righteousness." Guess who? Jesus is our righteousness. Through no good deed of our own, He did everything necessary to give us right standing with God. All we need to do is come to Him and surrender control of our lives to Him. Then the Father looks upon us as righteous not because of what we have done, but because of Jesus.

What a deal! Don't you want to love a God who gives you complete security forever, regardless of what anyone does to you and regardless of your many sins? Don't you want to love Him back? Don't you want to love others who love Him back? Don't you want to love everyone who doesn't yet love Him back? You are free to not care if anyone loves you back! Your chains are broken, no strings attached. You are stuck with Jesus and He is stuck with you! You need fear no man; You are free to love every man from His heart.

Do you want to be stuck with Jesus? Come rest from the world's oration. He will help you walk His talk.

Let us pray:

Father, so many times I have not treated every follower of Jesus as a beloved sister or brother in Your family. Regardless of their specific calling, help me love them without looking for anything back from them. Help me rest from oration. Train me to only speak Your truth in Your love to everyone around me. Amen.

JOY

Real Joy:
Continual Celebration

Plastic Joy:
Contingent Happiness

Chapter 8

What a Ride!

I have told you these things so that you will be filled with my joy. Yes, your joy will overflow!

—John 15:11

It was the first cold, rainy day of autumn. Everywhere people complained as if winter was breathing down their necks, a contagion of overreaction. In a few short months, January wind chills would make this day seem like a warm bath! However, the grousing continued throughout the Sam's Club parking lot when my wife Kim heard something. Turning to the sound she saw a man riding a bicycle through the downpour singing joyfully at the top of his lungs. He intermittingly continued the tune on his harmonica suspended before his mouth by a neck rack.

Kim couldn't help but smile wide. Laughter replaced griping throughout the parking lot. This is how the Lord wants His people to look to the world. They ride with the King. They ride above their circumstances with Him.

Happiness is merely an emotion dependent upon what *happens* to you. Real joy flows only from the Lord within you as you walk with Him. If you live for yourself and the world's agenda, you will occasionally find happiness but never a lasting joy. If you live for the Lord, He promises in Isaiah 58 to release an ever-flowing wellspring of His joyful Spirit within you.

For whom are you living? Are you following the world's agenda or the Lord? What really matters to the Lord? Are there any adjustments you need to make?

The choice is yours. Living a self-centered life chains you to fleeting moments of happiness spaced between long periods of discontent which only make you, and others around you, miserable. Resting in Jesus as the center of your life releases an ever flowing spring in good times and sad. He will make your life a constantly growing garden which will nourish other's lives.

Jesus waits for you with open arms. He is the only person who can provide you real lasting joy. Will you go through this life to the beat of your own drum? Or will you joyride in His one man band?

Let's pray:

Lord, I'm tired of my mood being dependent upon my circumstances. I only want to depend on You. Help me to fall in step with drumbeat of Your joyous heart. Lead on. Amen.

Chapter 9

Victory Shout!

The joy of the Lord is your strength.

—Nehemiah 8:10

Do you have a favorite picture hanging on your wall? My guess is that picture brings you some measure of happiness, maybe even real joy. Mine does. It hangs in a little pine paneled second-story room that leads up to the attic office of our ministry. We call it our "turn around room" because you enter it from our second-story hallway and turn around to go up the attic steps.

I could just as easily call it my "return to childhood room" because Kim has delightfully decorated it with a shelf of "retro" toys which hearken back to my childhood. At Christmas I act just like a little kid when my family and friends have given me these toys; G.I. Joe complete with footlocker, Rock-Em Sock-Em Robots, Skittle Bowl, a hand carved F16 fighter plane, an enlarged Sandy Koufax baseball card, metal checkers/Chinese checkers board, Beautiful Joe and Power Boys books, and a 64-pack of Crayola Crayons. There is no doubt I experience a sense of happiness when I pause and handle the toys. But joy awakens when I look at the picture on the wall. I'll tell you about the picture, but first a little background.

In the late winter of my son's junior year in high school, Kim and I felt led to move out of town and take a new pastoral assignment after nine very fruitful and tumultuous years at the new church we were serving. It was a difficult time for our family. Our daughter Emily was just finishing her first year at a local college and happily living at home as a commuter while interning at a local ministry. Our decision placed her in a position of making unanticipated decisions about new housing as her family moved away. College students usually move away from family, not vice versa. Very soon dear friends with whom Emily served in ministry opened their home to her. Praise the Lord!

We assured Daniel we would make arrangements for him to stay behind if he wanted. Relatives, friends, and even his football coach offered to take him in. He was a football star looking forward to his senior year and helping his team win a championship while being recruited by many universities. Even without football, no teenager wants to leave his friends, especially before senior year. We hated putting him in this position, but assumed he would stay behind, and planned accordingly. However, one late spring day Daniel told us, "If God is calling my parents to move to Marshalltown then I believe He is calling me to move with you. I want to be with my family my senior year."

It was a true life changing decision for Daniel in unhappy circumstances. Yet, the moment he told us, we all felt real joy welling up within us. What's really going on within us when joy rises?

We moved to Marshalltown and the Lord blessed Daniel with great favor. He was received by his ecstatic coaches with open arms. They recognized his abilities and character and gave him new freedom to roam the field on both offense and defense. It's not every day a 6'4" 300 pound high school player gets to catch passes and score touchdowns. More important, Daniel was warmly received by his teammates with genuine friendship. I am so grateful to the Lord for how He blessed my son in that time.

My first Sunday in the pulpit I announced we would beat the rival town school. It was quite a claim since Marshalltown had not defeated Newton for thirty-one years! Some thought the new preacher rather cocky; others chalked it up to a prejudiced dad. I didn't care. I just wanted to celebrate and encourage my son and his teammates. Life is too short not to celebrate and encourage. The team did in fact go on to have its first winning season in many years and we cheered happily as Daniel sacked quarterbacks, caught passes, scored his first touchdown, and made many game winning blocks and tackles. He became the first player from Marshalltown to win First Team All State honors in football and won a full scholarship to play at Western Illinois University. That Marshalltown team finished a breath away from the state playoffs and established a freewheeling style of play paving the way for many winning Marshalltown teams in succeeding years. The crowning achievement came in the last game of the year against Newton and the dreaded thirty-one-year "curse." The game on Newton's home field began with a massive rain storm that left the field a mud bath. The lead seesawed until Marshalltown's quarterback led a late drive passing with a wet ball with amazing precision to take the lead. Then it was time for the defense to hold the powerful running attack of Newton one last time. Newton had stayed in the game the second half by giving the ball almost every play to its star runner. Marshalltown finally stopped him when the coach gave Daniel the "green light" to line up on defense wherever he wanted to shadow the star runner. The strategy worked and Newton ran out of time, could not pass the ball, and Marshalltown prevailed with all our fans joining the team on the field for a delirious celebration of the end of the "curse."

The newspaper ran a photo the next day on the front page of Daniel—massive, red headed, muddy, rain soaked with outstretched arm holding his helmet in one hand and the other fist raised in the midst of an exultant victory shout. That photo is now blown up in a frame next to my shelf of retro toys. Every time I see the photo real joy rises up within me as I remember how the Lord guided and sustained my son, and the rest of us, in a challenging time of life transition. Yes, his football success brought emotional thrill and happiness but that's not what I'm talking about.

Every time I see the photo I'm reminded the joy of the Lord is my strength. When the Holy Spirit led Nehemiah to write this verse he used the Hebrew word for "joy" which literally means "shout of victory." Real joy is not a happy feeling because you won a contest. Real joy comes as a shout welling up deep within you declaring and reminding you that God is the victor!

Nehemiah was sent by God to lead the returned exiles from Babylon in rebuilding the walls of Jerusalem. They faced ridicule, sabotage, and death threats from the locals and divisiveness and despair in their own ranks. Working on the wall must have been as emotionally exhausting as it was inspiring. Several generations had passed as the exiles labored in captivity in Babylon. Indeed the joyous shout of victory went forth when God led the king of Babylon to allow the release and return of the captive generations of Jews to their homeland. However, the sight of desolated and completely destroyed Jerusalem must have been crushing. Working on the wall was a labor of faith where each Jew was constantly reminded of the destruction that came from Israel's past unfaithfulness.

Nehemiah knew their strength could not be found in the day to day circumstances of rebuilding the wall. He knew the people could only grow strong through the constant practice of shouting of God's past, present, and future victories—regardless of how they felt in the moment.

Real joy is found in shouting the victories of God. It's called praise. The apostle Paul has a word for it in the Bible.

Always be full of joy in the Lord. I say it again—rejoice! Philippians 4:4

Rejoice. It basically means to "re-joy"—to get back in touch with God's joy. "Rejoicing" is entering the "turn around room" to His heart. The Holy Spirit is always joyfully shouting the greatest victory shout of all, "Jesus is Lord!"

So I want you to know that no one speaking by the 'Spirit of God will curse Jesus, and no one can say Jesus is Lord except by the Holy Spirit. 1 Corinthians 12:4

The greatest victory ever won in the entire universe was won by Jesus. In His life, death, and resurrection Jesus defeated sin, the devil, and death FOREVER! All who put their trust in Jesus in this life are given ETERNAL VICTORY over sin, the devil, and death! If you have received Jesus as your Lord and Savior, then His victory IS YOURS! The Holy Spirit is always multi-tasking. As he lives in you one of the things He is always doing is the victory shout "Jesus is Lord!"

Rejoicing means you "re-join" with the victory shout of the Holy Spirit within you. It's as if there is constant white hot electrical current, like a continual bolt of lightning, firing deep within you. When you rejoice you take hold of the lightning.

You can keep striving and straining for your next momentary pleasurable experience or you can get into the daily habit of tapping into His wellspring of rejoicing.

No matter how down you are, no matter how bad your circumstance, you can enter the "turn around room" of your heart and shout out with the Holy Spirit, "Jesus, You are my victorious Lord!" Watch what happens. Shout it again. Stop worrying what anyone thinks. Shout it again. His joy will begin radiating from within you and strengthening you exactly as you need. When you rejoice you return to your true identity, your true childhood with your heavenly Father through Jesus. And guess what? The more you rejoice with His victory shout, the more lighthearted and childlike joy you will feel.

Our God is emotional and created you to have a full range of emotions. He is not against happy feelings, He loves them! The point is that real joy *is* victory shouting with Him which the Holy Spirit follows by stirring feelings of divine pleasure in you. The Lord wants you to be truly happy *with Him*. He wants the real fruit of joy to come forth. If you wait only when you feel happy about your circumstances to rejoice then you are going to miss out on continual joy. Remember Paul says rejoice *always*.

I am very thankful my son got to release a mud splattered victory shout on a night when he truly helped his team end a thirty-one-year football "curse." But every time I see that picture I'm reminded of the meaning of my son's name. He is Daniel

Richard. “Daniel” means “God is my vindicator.” “Richard” means “of the Lionheart.”

Therefore, every time I see that victorious picture, I am reminded Jesus died to break the curse of Sin, to vindicate me, and give me everlasting life with Him! I am reminded Jesus is the Lion of the tribe of Judah and roars with love in the jungle of life and no one threatens or defeats Him. You, Daniel, me, everyone has the opportunity to roar with Him forever.

Feeling down? Turn around. Shout victory. Roar. Rejoice always. Bear the continual fruit of joy. Jesus is Lord!

Let’s pray:

JESUS, YOU ARE AWESOME! AMEN!

Chapter 10

Hang Time

I am the vine; you are the branches. Whoever abides in me and I in him, he it is that bears much fruit, for apart from me you can do nothing. If anyone does not abide in me he is thrown away like a branch and withers; and the branches are gathered, thrown into the fire, and burned. If you abide in me, and my words abide in you, ask whatever you wish, and it will be done for you. By this my Father is glorified, that you bear much fruit and so prove to be my disciples. As the Father has loved me, so have I loved you. Abide in my love. If you keep my commandments, you will abide in my love, just as I have kept my Father's commandments and abide in his love. These things I have spoken to you, that my joy may be in you, and that your joy may be full.

—John 15:5-11 English Standard Version

In 1996, I experienced victorious joy in worshiping Jesus with 70,000 men at a Promise Keepers event at Soldier Field Football Stadium in Chicago. I treasure many memories: singing to Jesus, men opening up to Jesus, four men in one room with broken air conditioning on a 100 degree day, and fire hoses cooling men off as we took our box lunches outside toward Lake Michigan.

I especially treasure being on my face with my beloved brother Steve as he rededicated his life to Jesus.

I will never forget the closing ceremony. Coach Bill McCartney called all the pastors down to the front. Though we were all imperfect shepherds we were also beloved by the Good Shepherd. Seventy thousand brothers in Christ gave us a ten minute roaring ovation and joined Bill in prayer for us. It was a little glimpse of the joy that waits in heaven for all who abide and bear fruit in Jesus.

Jesus is speaking intimately to you right now from John 15. It's as simple as 1-2-3.

1. If you dwell daily in Him…
2. If you daily fill yourself with His words
3. You'll get what you ask, bear fruit, and *be* joyful.

"Abiding" in Him means to make your abode or home in Him. It means you choose moment by moment to stick close. It means you see each day as a series of moments to receive and give love with Him and others. Do you want this? If you draw close to Him, He will draw close to you.

Come close to God, and God will come close to you. Wash your hands, you sinners; purify your hearts, for your loyalty is divided between God and the world. James 4:8

A simple teaching given that hot day in Chicago is seared into my mind. A speaker said, "I'm sure all you dads would say you love your children. However, dads, when it comes to loving your children here is how you spell love—T-I-M-E!" The whole "quality time" concept is another "plastic fruit" cop-out for all of us who over-commit to things the Lord never calls us to, and under-commit to the things He does.

Quantity *is* quality! You show your love for your spouse, children, and friends by how much time you spend with them. You show your love for the Lord by how much time you spend with Him. He shows you how much He loves you by dying for your sins, rising for your eternal life, and sending the Holy Spirit to woo you to Him so He can live in you—with you at all times. He is with you and me always. But sadly we are not always with Him and this is the biggest practical cause of the famine of love.

Abiding is being *with* Him. In fact, the more you are with Him alone, the more He can help you be with Him as you are with others. That's when things get really fruitful. In verse 7, Jesus spells out how He wants you to be with Him alone so that He can guide you to be with Him at all times.

If you abide in me, and my words abide in you, ask whatever you wish, and it will be done for you. John 15:7 NKJV

When you choose to spend *serious* time filling your soul with His living words from Scripture then your prayers will yield real results.

Soldier Field is the home of the Chicago Bears football team. I have long enjoyed watching my favorite team, the Green Bay Packers, battle the archrival Bears. In 2011, the Pack won a hard fought game at Soldier Field propelling them to a Super Bowl victory over the Pittsburgh Steelers. Yes, the "Pack is Back." That phrase hearkens the glory days of the Packers in the 1960s with Vince Lombardi. Their punter was a versatile running back named Donnie Anderson. He did not punt the ball longer than others, but he did punt it much *higher*. This stopped the opponent from running the ball back very far. Anderson's punts were a strategy that was given a new name in football culture—"hang time."

Abiding with Jesus as the Vine requires you and me to spend more "hang time." The more one-on-one time you spend with Him the higher your joy, the more you will help people, and the more you will destroy the devil's plans.

The Lord longs for you to hang out with Him constantly throughout each day and the first step is to begin each day alone with Him. This is His time tested, much testified, way. It may not be your way, but it's His way. Is he worth it? Let Him take you higher.

Give attention to the sound of my cry, my King and my God, for to you do I pray. O LORD, in the morning you hear my voice; in the morning I prepare a sacrifice for you and watch. For you are not a God who delights in wickedness; evil may not dwell with you. Psalm 5:2-4 ESV

At this moment you may be painfully aware of how little time you spend alone with Him. Stop hanging your head in shame or fear. Look up to Him right now. He's not pointing a finger at you. He's simply opening His arms. He is not dwelling on your faults, He's dwelling *in you*! So dwell with Him.

You've captured my heart, dear friend. You looked at me, and I fell in love. One look my way and I was hopelessly in love! Song of Solomon 4:9, The Message

Every look from you captures His heart, like any true Daddy, like any true Lover of your soul. That day at Soldier Field, we saw men become real men when they loved Jesus passionately. Real breakthroughs come when we see the Song of Solomon as a picture of how Jesus loves Israel and each believer in Christ.

If you have given your life to Jesus then you are part of the Bride. The young man in the Song represents Jesus and the young woman represents you, me, and every believer. The Lord knows exactly what He won for us on the cross and how He wants men and women to abide in His love.

What joy we often forfeit when we spend so much time feeling shame because we don't spend enough time with Him! Such shame keeps us from coming to Him. Instead, just look back to Him. It's a mystery of His amazing grace, but He spends His time savoring the last time you captured His heart and deeply anticipating the next time you look to Him. If you let Him, He will teach you to never look away at all. John Wesley called it constant communion.

The Lord wants to help you learn to abide in Him at all times. The more you hang out with Him, the more you will become like Him, the more you will start praying for the things He wants, the more He will give you the things He wants for you!

You do not have, because you do not ask. You ask and do not receive, because you ask wrongly, to spend it on your passions. James 4:2-3 ESV

One reason you do not receive what you want from the Lord is you are not asking and then trusting Him for it. Another reason is because you are asking with the wrong motive. He sees your heart at all times. He wants your heart resting deeply in Him. Then he can cleanse your heart of wrong desires and fill your heart with His desires. When you start praying according to His desires and His word He will be glad to give you everything you ask. Faith, healing and miracles will increase the higher your "hang time."

Two things will keep you from growing in constant companionship with Jesus: not asking Him to help you, and doubting that He will. You must unlearn your "unabiding" ways and practice His ways. He will help you. Do you want it?

He promises your life will be constantly overflowing with real joy if you keep hanging out with Him, feasting on His words, and praying with Him for results.

These things I have spoken to you, that my joy may be in you, and that your joy may be full. John 15:11 ESV

How much do you want a joy filled life? Come to Him right now as you reflect on some important questions.

How much T-I-M-E do you spend resting with your Best Friend daily in quiet *centering prayer*?

How much T-I-M-E do you spend listening with your heart to your Best Friend daily in *meditating on Scripture*?

How much T-I-M-E do you spend praying with your Best Friend daily in *Spirit-led prayer for others and yourself?*

How much T-I-M-E do you spend looking into a phone, computer screen, television, newspaper, magazine, or book? I'm not saying any one of these things is necessarily bad, but they often represent the best the world has to offer in "plastic fruit."

Take inventory *with* the Lord. Let Him prune these unhelpful things away and increase your time with Him.

Proverbs says that people are unrestrained and perish without vision from the Lord. We all stumble the moment we take our eyes off of Him and look to other things not worthy of Him.

When people do not accept divine guidance, they run wild. But whoever obeys the law is joyful. Proverbs 29:18

But the moment we get our hearts back on him, here comes the Joy. There are many ways to hang out with Him, feast upon

His words, and pray with Him for results. In Chapter 25, I will outline one way that works for me and for many. Go for it!

At any given moment, you and I are either growing closer to Him or farther away. The stakes are high. Life is not a football game.

If anyone does not abide in me he is thrown away like a branch and withers; and the branches are gathered, thrown into the fire, and burned. John 15:6 ESV

For you, and the people around you, it's a matter of real life and death. Increase your hang time. Apart from Him you can do nothing. Abiding in Him you can do everything that matters.

He was hung on a tree for your eternal life. Will you hang with Him? The Great Promise Keeper, the Great Joy Giver awaits your decision.

PEACE

Real Peace:
His Assuring Presence

Plastic Peace:
Absence of Conflict

CHAPTER 11

DIFFERENCE MAKER

For the LORD corrects those he loves, just as a father corrects a child in whom he delights.

—Proverbs 3:12

One early spring day my wife and I were enjoying a cup of coffee in our sitting room overlooking two neighborhood backyards. I noticed two small neighbor children gleefully coming out to play with their brand new baseball gloves, caps, and ball. Little sister's cap and glove were matching pink! Big brother immediately began throwing too hard to little sister who had no chance of catching it. She would then run all the way to the back fence to retrieve the ball and run back to launch a high arching throw over his outstretched arms. She was a strong armed five-year-old lefty!

I chuckled and said to my wife, "Kim, watch these two playing catch." After witnessing this process repeat itself Kim remarked, "They're not playing 'catch,' they're playing 'throw'"!

Soon big brother was throwing even harder with little sister rapidly losing interest. With a rising level of frustration and distraction she lackadaisically wandered toward the far corner only to be startled through the fence by the barking of the onrushing neighbor dog. By now, big brother had turned away in disgust beating the ground with a newfound stick. Things were degenerating.

Just then, their dad came out of the house with his own glove and they both perked up. He immediately told each child where to stand as the three formed three points of a triangle. He saw to it that little sister was positioned twice as close to him as big brother. Then he threw underhanded to little sister so she could catch it consistently. Each time you could see her confidence building as she was now motivated to focus her throws on a more direct trajectory to Dad.

Dad threw over-handed to big brother at a reasonable speed proving his dad knew he could handle more than his sister. At first, Dad only allowed the kids to throw to him. After their confidence and focus increased, then he allowed them to throw occasionally to each other. He instructed big brother to throw underhanded to little sister, just like him. Suddenly everything was regenerating and we could tell what a big deal it was for both children. Their body language said "This is awesome!" Funny thing, they must have played catch together as a threesome for twenty minutes with no frustration.

The real God of peace wants us to play joyfully and justly. We can't do it without His assuring presence. We may begin with new equipment and great intentions, but left to ourselves we degenerate in pride, distraction, frustration, and harm. We either draw upon His peace or we end up in pieces.

Jesus called God "Abba" which means "Daddy." When Daddy is present *and* listened to, good things happen—it's a big deal! He knows our weaknesses and potential. He knows how to position us for success. He knows how much to stretch us. He always has our best interest at heart. He corrects us, not because He doesn't want us to have fun, but because He loves us and wants our lives to be truly fruitful.

Every one of us has a need to be loved and guided by a parent we trust. God put that need in us hoping we will let Him be our perfect Father through a relationship with Jesus.

There is a famine of real parenting love in the world because we have settled for relativism rather than relationship with the Real God of the Ten Commandments. Many parents don't let the Lord lead them according to Scripture in their own secret life so they fearfully and guiltily shrink back from loving younger generations enough to point them to absolute, eternal truths.

Yet, Jesus keeps opening His arms inviting us to come to Him saying, "I am the way, the truth, and the life. No one comes to the Father except by Me." Jesus loves us enough to tell us the truth. He knows that He is what is best for us. There are real absolutes. The greatest absolute is that the God who made you loves you so much He died for your sins to offer you eternal life.

Real peace comes only from a present Father who knows how to help us grow and live together in love.

What will it be? Degeneration or regeneration? Peace or pieces? Throw away the gift or get caught up in His presence?

He can make all the difference between "throw" and "catch."

Chapter 12

Take Heart

I have said these things to you that in me you may have peace. In the world you will have tribulation. But take heart, I have overcome the world.

—John 16:33 ESV

I am a sucker for happy endings. I will often shout, pump my fist, or cry every time the good guy wins at the end of a book or movie. In fact, I won't watch or read fiction if I'm told ahead it has an unhappy ending. Some say that is unrealistic. Yet, it is unrealistic, cynical, and despairing to pretend that life is ultimately painful, dark, and dirty. That's living a lie.

So much literature and media is full of brokenness, immorality, and darkness—yet most all-time favorites show good triumphing over evil. Why? God has given everyone the ability to recognize good and evil and a longing for good to triumph over evil.

Our human nature is distorted by sin to be sure and therefore we often twist and confuse good with evil. Nonetheless, there is emptiness in each person that only God can fill. There is only one way that a human life can have a triumphant ending and destiny. All history is *His*-story—the greatest true story ever told. Everyone one who ends up *in* Him will live happily ever after, Amen! This is ultimate realism.

Read the last chapter of the Bible in the book of Revelation. God wins, Jesus reigns forever and ever, Amen!

When my children were young, Friday night was often pizza and movie night. When a scene became suspenseful, with the good guy in mortal danger, the kids would cry out, "Mommy, Mommy is he going to die?" At that point I would tap the pause button.

You notice they asked their mom. The first time they asked me I told them to just relax and experience the movie. That didn't cut it. They needed to know the happy ending ahead of time *so* they could relax. Kim knew this and would simply tell them the ending. At first this frustrated me, but then I realized that my beloved children *needed* reassurance that good would triumph.

We all need that reassurance. That's why Jesus says, "Take heart, I have overcome the world."

He first said this to his disciples the night before he died. They must have found this hard to believe since his public support had waned and the religious establishment was becoming increasingly hostile. The disciples must have found his "take heart" statement impossible to understand after he was tortured and died the next day, an apparent failure.

The Holy Spirit led John to first write of this amazing pronouncement sixty years after Jesus was raised from the dead. Early Christians were beginning to receive intense persecution from the Roman Empire. The Holy Spirit knew it was just the right time for believers to be reassured that Jesus had overcome every threat they would ever face. They could overcome because the Overcomer lived in them!

Do you find it hard to believe and receive Jesus' "take heart" words right now? The Holy Spirit knows it's just the right time for you to hear this. If you have received Jesus as your Lord, then deep down at the core of your being He is your peace. You are a person of peace. It's just that you don't always feel calm. That's because real peace is His presence in you, not the plastic peace of a calm feeling.

Sister Therese, a Franciscan nun, was a dear friend and a great spiritual encouragement to me. She always welcomed me with a big hug and bright smile. She had been through much and you could tell she savored every present moment with each precious person. She would take my coat and bring out a tea chest filled with great variety. The hot water was ready and so was Therese. She would deeply listen to me share my inner spiritual life for almost an hour. Then we would listen quietly to the Holy Spirit and she would pray deeply as He would speak to my heart through her. It might be just a phrase or verse or simple suggestion for pondering and bright light would flood my soul.

One day, with her eyes closed, she said, "Deep down at the core of your being I see a bedrock of peace. Above that bedrock there is sometimes unrest but deep down the Spirit is saying all is well."

Later that afternoon I walked alone in the woods and felt the Lord speak in my heart, "I have made you my man of peace, yet you often practice recreational anxiety." It was pretty hilarious and convicting. So often I would stew about something, when deep down I had a sense that all would be well. There is nothing re-creative about worry. Worry is a destructive lack of trust in a

God who is always working for our good. The Lord asked me to find one place in Scripture where it says He is ever worried. I realized for the first time in my life He never worries about what I worry about. It was a life changing perspective.

It's always your choice. Feel overwhelmed or trust the Overcomer. He is not threatened by whatever threatens you. He has already defeated it. He hurts with you in your worry, but He's ready to receive that burden if you will surrender it.

You are loved more than you know. You are more secure in that love than you feel. Take heart. Plastic peace comes from trying hard to whip yourself into the calm of psychological certainty. Real peace comes from "taking heart," no matter how you feel. Taking heart means simply taking Him at His word. When you do, He fills your heart with His heart. The Holy Spirit helps you to become sensitive to what He sees, knows, and feels every present moment. All of a sudden you will realize, regardless of the situation, you are standing on solid rock.

Whatever is going on in the world right now, here is how it ends: the Good Guy died *and* reigns evermore.

Now relax and enjoy the rest of the "movie."

Chapter 13

Warrior Prince

So everyone who acknowledges me before men, I also will acknowledge before my Father who is in heaven, but whoever denies me before men, I also will deny before my Father who is in heaven. "Do not think that I have come to bring peace to the earth. I have not come to bring peace, but a sword. For I have come to set a man against his father, and a daughter against her mother, and a daughter-in-law against her mother-in-law. And a person's enemies will be those of his own household. Whoever loves father or mother more than me is not worthy of me, and whoever loves son or daughter more than me is not worthy of me. And whoever does not take his cross and follow me is not worthy of me. Whoever finds his life will lose it, and whoever loses his life for my sake will find it.

—Matthew 10:32-39 ESV

Take a moment to slowly reread Jesus' words above. He doesn't exactly make you feel calm, does he? That's because His peace comes from piercing.

In 1980, I was twenty-three and attending seminary training to be a pastor. One of the toughest and most enlightening classes I took was an advanced course on the Gospel of Matthew under

Dominican professor Benedict Viviano. He was a brilliant scholar who demanded rigorous preparation of his students, but also had a caring heart for everyday Christians seeking to follow Jesus. Our assignment was to write a research paper on a passage of our choice from the book of Matthew. However, there was one catch—we had to pick a passage that troubled us, where Jesus said something we didn't like, something we would rather ignore. Brother Benedict wanted us to become honest and faithful teachers of the Scripture whose lives were shaped by Scripture, not lazy preachers who only taught their opinions twisting Scripture to their own purposes. The assignment changed my life.

My favorite t-shirt at the time said "Give peace a chance," reminiscent of John Lennon's war protest song. The Cold War, Vietnam, and Watergate caused many in my generation to distrust our government and elevate "world peace" to top priority. "Peace" as absence of conflict became prized at all costs. As a history major, one would think I had learned violent opposition and preparedness is unfortunately necessary when opposing evil men and systems led by men such as Hitler, Stalin, Mao, Hussein, Achminijihad, and Bin Laden.

In Matthew 10, it became clear to me that Jesus wants to dispel any worldly notions of peace. Real peace is not worldwide absence of conflict. That is a pipe dream which ignores the sinful nature of humanity. The Prince of Peace is a Warrior King who came to fight and win for us something deeper and everlasting. He defies all attempts to co-opt Him for our own agendas. He is not running for President. He is the King. He isn't interested in popularity; He's out to save the population. He doesn't have to be diplomatic, but bluntly declares anyone who denies Him will be denied by Him in the next life. He's not here to give us a peaceful easy feeling. He came to give us eternal life and rest from the enemy. He knows the devil and our sin nature. That's why He came to bring a sword.

Let us therefore strive to enter that rest, so that no one may fall by the same sort of disobedience. For the word of God is living and active, sharper than any two-edged sword, piercing to the division of soul and of spirit, of joints and of marrow, and discerning the thoughts and intentions of the heart. And no creature is hidden from his sight, but all are naked and exposed to the eyes of him to whom we must give account. Hebrews 4:11-13 ESV

He does not force us to choose Him. He does force us to decide. There is no middle ground. He loves us too much for that. He came to divide us from evil with a relentless love that will ultimately save all who come to Him and ultimately destroy all who will not. He knows our worldly theologies and philosophies of peace and humanism actually aids satanic oppression of billions. He is intolerant of sin because sin hurts people He so loves. He loves us enough to cause conflicts between family members and nations if that's what it takes to get everyone's attention. He knows He is the only thing that eternally matters to every precious soul. He is a loving divider to help us become trusting deciders.

Jesus came as the Living Word to cut through all personal and worldly sin straight to every person's heart. He came to die for sin that all who trust Him would find real peace, shalom. "Shalom" is the Hebrew word which is often translated as "peace" but it actually means peace that comes with right relationship with God. Something only Jesus can give. Peace is not so much a feeling, but the relationship we are given. Jesus gives us peace with the Father.

These things I have spoken to you while I am still with you. But the Helper, the Holy Spirit, whom the Father will send in my name, he will teach you all things and bring to your remembrance all that I have said to you. Peace I leave with you; my peace I give to you. Not as the world gives do I give to you. Let not your hearts be troubled, neither let them be afraid. John 14:25-27 ESV

Real peace isn't realized until you come to Jesus and He gives it to you. Real peace is the companionship of the Holy Spirit.

Still, we would rather have peace on our own terms. When most people live long enough they finally agree that the world is an unfriendly place where conflict is unavoidable. However, many will nonetheless pursue their own "peace of mind" as an escape, rather than do it the Lord's way.

Then David comforted Bathsheba, his wife, and slept with her. She became pregnant and gave birth to a son, and they named him Solomon. The Lord loved the child and sent word through Nathan the prophet that his name should be Jedidiah—"beloved of the Lord"—because the Lord loved him. 2 Samuel 12:24-25

King David loved God with all his heart yet made a horrible choice. He arranged the death of Bathsheba's husband Uriah, his loyal friend, so he could take Bathsheba as his own. God confronted him through the prophet Nathan, and David repented. (Sometime read David's prayer of repentance in Psalm 51. If you ever blow it, pray that prayer with all your heart and watch real peace come!)

Though God forgave him, David experienced the painful consequences of his choices. After the death of the child conceived in his adulterous affair with Bathsheba, David took her in as one of his wives. They named their next child Solomon, which means "peaceable." They were declaring, "We've been through a lot, but maybe we can have a little peace." They were like most people today hoping for mere survival and maybe a little peace. It's the best the world hopes for and the best the world can offer; plastic fruit.

But Jesus offers so much more.

Notice "*they* named him Solomon," but the *Lord* named him "Jedidiah"—"beloved of the Lord." As long as Solomon found his identity in being beloved, he became the wise king. But when he found his identity in being the wise king, he was given over to idolatry. When you find your identity in what you do, your security depends upon your performance; but when you find your identity in *being loved by the Lord*, your security depends upon *His* performance—you find yourself filled with peace because you are in right relationship with the Lord. I call this the Jedidiah Identity—overflowing with the peace of His presence. You are his beloved. Resting in that truth brings real peace.

Please understand, this real peace must be fought for. Hebrews 4 says, "strive to enter into His rest." You pick up your cross and follow Jesus in His way, His words, and His love which cuts through all the junk! It means you don't settle for the false peace your friends and family may seek. They may notice something different about you and not like it. Don't take the bait and lash out if they tease you or lash out at you. Instead, pray for them. Ask the Lord to give you more of His heart for them. Ask Him to set up opportunities to tell them what Jesus is doing for you. They may try to pull you back into seeking peace of mind in worldly ways that are not fruitful. Many things people do for "recreation" that are not recreative!

The only source of real peace of mind is the Holy Spirit inside you. The only way the Holy Spirit comes to live inside you is if you receive Jesus as your Lord and Savior. If you have Jesus then you have peace. If you don't have Jesus, no amount of recreation, alcohol, exercise, nature walks, money or fame will ever satisfy.

Peace is something you cannot acquire with external leisure. Peace is something you fight on the inside to receive. If you choose to pick up your cross in prayer and battle against worry, peace will be given to you from within by the Holy Spirit.

Be anxious for nothing, but in everything by prayer and supplication, with thanksgiving, let your requests be made known to God; and the peace of God, which surpasses all understanding, will guard your hearts and minds through Christ Jesus. Philippians 4:6-7 NKJV

The next time you are tempted to worry, cast it all on Him. Pray aloud according to Philippians 4 like this:

Stop worrying, start praying.

Thank the Lord for everything that comes to mind. (Thank Him for making you. Thank Him for loving you. Thank Him for dying on the cross for you. The Holy Spirit within you will remind you of things.)

Make your request.

(Pour out your whole heart and "ask big." Ask the Lord to fix every single thing you were worried about. Before you know it the Holy Spirit inside you will release His peace like a force field guarding your heart and mind in a way that cannot be explained.

Thank Him for the unexplainable peace He is releasing.

His peace guards you because life is a war. The way you give real peace a chance is to follow your Warrior King. The more you pray, the more peace you will receive, the more peaceful you will be in all your relationships, the more others will want the peace you've found.

Jesus is the world's only hope of real peace. Fight alongside Him!

PATIENCE

Real Patience: Waiting for What He Wants

Plastic Patience: Waiting for What I Want

Chapter 14

Taking Care of Business

I will contend with those who contend with you, and I will save your children.

—Isaiah 49:25 ESV

My wife Kim once said to me, "Sweetheart, you know I love you dearly, but if I was ever threatened in a dark alley, I would much rather have your brother with me than you." So much for my male ego, but, I had to agree.

When we were growing up my brother was the fighter and I was the talker. I was four years older and won all our scuffles for years. But there came a time as young men when I realized my little brother could beat me up. I saw to it we never had a fight after that! My brother Steve is a great guy with a big heart always ready to help anyone down and out with the shirt off his back. He's also great to have in your corner against a bully. That's just the way he is, tenderhearted and tough—as needed.

However, once when he was a teenager a gang of bullies came after him. Things didn't look good. Then word on the street reached a longtime friend of mine.

My friend Doug was the quietest and toughest of my hometown friends. He was the oldest of five, grew up on the tough side of town, letting his actions speak loudly. He was a top flight wrestler and we knew he would have been state champion except his family situation demanded he work instead. Doug rarely spoke his mind, loved his Cincinnati Reds baseball team (The Big Red Machine of the 1970s who were always beating my Dodgers), and greatly enjoyed a beer while listening to his favorite group, Bachman Turner Overdrive, play such songs as "Taking Care of Business." Doug was loyal, big hearted, and very, very tough. We all knew he was no one to mess with—ever.

When Doug learned my brother was in trouble, he did not hesitate and passed word to the leader of the bullies to leave "little Stevie" alone. The bully had learned long before to not mess with Doug. Doug let him know whoever touched Steve would answer to him. That's all it took. No more threat. No more fear. Doug had quietly "taken care of business."

Bullying comes in many forms. Years later my brother was visiting us when I was a young preacher. We had just experienced powerful worship and I was feeling great when I went to my office and found the first nasty anonymous letter I had ever received. I was stewing over it when I arrived home for Sunday dinner. My brother saw the look on my face and asked what was wrong. I handed him the letter. He read it and simply said, "From now on this is what you do with such letters." He wadded it up, mimicked using the letter like toilet paper, and threw it in the trash! It wasn't very religious, but it was deeply spiritual! I burst out laughing and the Lord lifted my burden. That's one lighthearted example of how my brother has blessed and protected me. Life is too short to let bullies have their way.

Real patience means letting the Lord contend with those who contend with you. You do this by praying and waiting before you allow someone to rob your joy; waiting before you strike back; waiting before you hold a grudge; waiting before you start hating yourself; waiting before you start pitying yourself; waiting while you seek help and counsel from fellow believers; waiting before you hold a grudge against the Lord even though you don't understand His purpose in allowing bad things to happen. Patience is waiting on the Lord. The Lord plays bullies for fools. Satan is a bully. He thrives on lies and fearful threats. Satan is terrified of Jesus Christ. Satan wants nothing to do with the Lord.

Satan is the accuser of the brethren, but Christ is the first born of many brethren! The Lord is not pointing a finger at you; He is opening His arms inviting you to come rest in His protective love. You are loved more than you know. You are more secure in His love than you may often feel. Insecure *feelings* are at the root of false patience.

False patience is when we convince ourselves we have waited long enough for the Lord to act and it's somehow okay to do His job for Him. We justify our need to resolve the uncomfortable uncertainty of the present situation and fight for ourselves on our own terms. We might look around for a comforting friend to affirm us for waiting as long as we have and agree that enough is enough. Real patience is an expression of real love to the Lord. False patience is when you wait longer than you think most people would wait and always involves self-justification often spilling into self-deception.

Bold decisiveness is not wrong. In fact, the Lord wants you to be decisive, continually deciding to boldly follow Him at all times! "Following" Him means deciding to be led. That's why He invites every human to take three very decisive steps every day.

Come to Me... take My yoke... learn from Me... you will find rest for your souls. Matthew 11:28-29 NKJV

These three action steps really comprise "Christianity 101." There is no "201." If you do these three things in your walk with the Lord every day, He will grow His real fruit in your Life, and you will end the famine of love around you. Jesus invites you to come exchange you burdens for the fullness of a personal relationship (His yoke) and learn *from* Him on His mission to save the lost.

Real patience means *decisively resting* from running your own life moment by moment, day by day. Real patience is bold! You continually come to the Lord with the bullying burden of whatever is threatening you and let Him put his arm around you and teach you how to go through it *with* Him. When you wait for the Lord to fight your battles and instruct your heart along the way, you are showing your trust and love for Him *even* though you don't feel like waiting any longer.

I'm still learning this myself. Though I'm the "Come Rest Guy," my heart still instinctively reacts in unrest when my loved ones are threatened. I am so grateful the Lord is a much more patient teacher than I am a learner!

When you receive Jesus as Lord and Savior you are no longer a slave to your sin nature. However your sin nature is never eradicated in this life; you always have to deal with it. The question is will you let the Lord control your sin nature or not? That's why Jesus says, "*Learn from* Me." We each have much to learn about letting the Spirit lead us by the heart when threatened rather than letting our sin nature lead us around by the nose. We will continue to experience intermittent pain and fear in this life. The Bible says only at the end of time will every tear be wiped away. But the Lord *is* with us along the way.

When you instinctively react with fear upon hearing threatening news, you will be immediately tempted toward impatience. Satan uses fear to bully us into sinfully worrisome thinking, hurtful words, and damaging actions. Yet, the Lord is always near saying, "Come rest in My love… learn from Me." So, when threatened about family, finances, the future, etc. go to the toughest Friend you have.

My son's coaches gave me the honor of praying with the team in the locker room before each home game. I remember the Spirit leading me to pray like this, "Lord Jesus, you are the toughest Man who ever lived. You took nails and a spear in your body and died on a cross for each one of us. We honor you tonight and pray as you taught…" We then prayed the Lord's Prayer together. It was very moving to honor the Lord as the toughest man who ever lived.

If you love Jesus, then His Dad is your Dad and can whip every pretender dad on the block. Wait on Him. Give Him time to take care of business. Pray out loud His promise from Isaiah 49:25. After you pray this verse, ask the Lord if there is truly anything He wants you to do besides trusting Him in prayer. He may bring a bold loving action to mind that has nothing to do with fear or pride. If so, do it. If not, sit tight. Either way, you are boldly following His lead.

The main thing is to decide to let Him do His job and keep his promise. If you belong to Christ, then you have been grafted into every promise God has made in the Bible to Israel. You can trust that, because of the blood of Jesus over your life, your Heavenly Father will defeat your bullies and He will save your children His way, not yours. He has never lost a fight, even on the cross, even after the cross. He paid the devil's ransom price and descended into hell and made the devil release hostage humanity so that now every human who calls on Jesus will be saved. Our awesome God is no one to mess with. Rest from worrying about your life. Focus on His business. He will take care of yours.

Let us pray:

"Lord Jesus, you are my friend and the toughest Man who ever lived. You know my fears and my bullies. I place them in Your hands. Show me what, if anything, you want me to do. Otherwise, I now declare and receive Your promise. You will contend with those who contend with me and You will save my children. Amen."

Chapter 15
The Thief's Promise

Understand this: If a homeowner knew exactly when a burglar was coming, he would keep watch and not permit his house to be broken into. You also must be ready all the time, for the Son of Man will come when least expected.

—Matthew 24:43-44

I awoke in the middle of a very still, pleasant summer night, 3:20 a.m. to be exact. Got up for awhile and went back to bed. Falling back into sleep I could plainly hear footsteps outside our window on the sidewalk below. We live in a two-story cottage with our bedroom overlooking our driveway and garage. However, the footsteps sounded too clear and close to me in my drowsiness to seem real. So I chose to shrug it off and yield to luxurious slumber.

Suddenly, it was as if someone tapped me and yanked at my t-shirt. I shot out of bed and opened the blinds to look down upon our two vehicles in the driveway. The dome light was on in our car with a dark figure just leaving and approaching the van. Remembering my van was unlocked, I barked, "HEY!!" The prowler froze, looked up in my direction, and nervously said something like, "Hey man, my bad, just wondering if you have any pans!" How absurd! At least that's what I thought he said.

Without deliberation, I screamed, "GET OUTTA HERE!!" My wife rose up from sleep screaming in terror and the young man bolted out into the street. I watched him for a moment as he made his way up the block while I tried to calm my wife with a profuse apology! With adrenalin pumping, knowing he was gone, I went downstairs and "boldly" went outside in my underwear to look over my "territory" and lock the van.

Later, upon wide awake reflection, I realized the young man was asking about "cans" instead of "pans." (Our state requires a deposit on cans making them a valuable find to the desperate.) It's possible he was telling the truth. It's possible he wasn't. More important, I realized I had greatly overreacted in fear, greatly "under reacted" in love by speaking to this human being like I would a stray dog.

Not exactly a highlight of my life's journey! Hearing a thief's footsteps in the night I impatiently responded by "protecting" our fifteen-year-old jalopy (the man no doubt needed the car worse than us), terrifying my wife (jeopardizing my own hide!), and treating a man worse than a dog (even a dog deserves better!) Real macho, but not real love!

Patient waiting upon the Lord might have given me an opportunity to witness to, or pray for, that desperate soul. I have since repented, asked the Lord to save that man, and if possible, give me another opportunity someday to make amends. I have also asked the Lord to help me lean on Him a lot more the next time I hear footsteps in the night. There is already too much fearful instinct driving human relations on the planet.

My lasting impression from that experience is the strikingly clear sound of the footsteps in the night. It's strangely reassuring. Strange enough to be the Lord Himself saying that He is giving humankind final preparation for His second coming.

"For you know quite well that the day of the Lord's return will come unexpectedly, like a thief in the night." 1 Thessalonians 5:2

You don't have to worry about when He returns. Those who draw close and walk with Him in this life will recognize the sound of his footsteps at His return.

The Bible says that at the right time in history, Christ died a thief's death for all of us ungodly people. Jesus is the Greatest Thief because He broke into the sinful world, Satan's house, and stole imprisoned humanity away. The Lord is now waiting patiently with love and has promised He will return when we expect it least and need it most.

The Lord isn't really being slow about his promise, as some people think. No, he is being patient for your sake. He does not want anyone to be destroyed, but wants everyone to repent. 2 Peter 3:9

So let the Holy Spirit control your fearful instincts and grow your patience with people around you. They may be stumbling in the dark for mere cans from you when they really need to find real gold *in* you.

Follow in the Thief's footsteps. You'll hear them soon enough.

Chapter 16

A Longer Fuse

The LORD is gracious and merciful; Slow to anger and great in lovingkindness.

—Psalm 145:8 NASB

It was the 4th of July in the summer of my fifteenth year. My new friend Dave was staying overnight. We had enjoyed the evening walking around our end of town blowing off firecrackers impressing one another with our macho bravado and one-upmanship in mischief. It was time to settle in for the night. My parents said goodnight in our little 800 sq. ft house and we shut my bedroom door.

We were about to shut the lights out for sleep when I decided to commit one last impressive act. I said, "Watch this!" I then pulled out a little firecracker so small that its fuse was twice its length. Our bedroom had two twin beds. Dave was in my brother's bed and I was sitting on my bed. I smiled and pulled out a book of matches. Dave seemed surprised. I struck the match. Dave seemed alarmed. I lit the fuse. Dave jumped back.

My plan was to light the extremely long fuse and then pinch it off with my fingers, to take us to the very edge of explosion before extinguishing. That was the plan. However, I had never actually tried this before. It just seemed to make sense that the fuse was long enough to avert the unthinkable. But when I went to pinch the lit fuse the first time it didn't go out. Dave's eyes grew wide. In succeeding split seconds I frantically tried two more times to pinch the fuse to no avail. At that moment, Dave flung himself against the wall side of his bed and covered his head.

Ka-boom! The firecracker exploded just as I instinctively released it from my hand. In a little house where all the windows are shut due to air conditioning—the littlest of firecrackers makes the loudest of noise! The last thing I saw before I leapt to shut out the light was a charred hole in the bed sheet and my charred fingers reaching for the light switch. Then we waited.

Out of my parents' bedroom at the back of the house came my dad lumbering like a bear out of slumber. I heard him shout something like "What the heck is going on!" I prepared. He opened the door and turned on the light and said, "What was that? It sounded like an explosion!" I lied, "Yeah Dad, some car just drove up and they threw an M-80 just outside our window! It shook the house!" I wasn't lying about that! An M-80 is almost like a small stick of dynamite and in his sleepy stupor my dad bought the lie. He said, "Well alright, now everybody settle down and go to sleep!" He shut the light off and began to walk back to his bedroom. My little brother was on the couch in the living room and was temporarily disappointed that big brother was apparently going to get away with this when suddenly my dad woke up enough and exclaimed, "Wait a minute, I smell smoke!"

Unfortunately for my desperate deceit, gunpowder smoke was now wafting all through the house. Suffice it to say there was another explosion. Dad and Mom rushed into our room as the light exposed charred remains of the bed sheet, firecracker fragments, and two cowering former "tough guys." As I confessed and apologized I broke into tears in my mother's forgiving arms. So much for impressing my new friend! Yes, my little brother was exultant! Prideful big brother's scheme was literally up in smoke. The fuse was not long enough.

I couldn't stop laughing while writing this which is a sign of the Lord's merciful healing all those years ago. For after all is said and done, the thing I remember most is crying forgiven in my mother's arms.

It is said that some people have a longer fuse than others which means that some are slower to lose their temper and explode in anger. You have your natural tendency and I have mine. No one is as slow as the Lord. No one has a longer fuse.

Refraining from exploding in human anger is prized as patience by the world. It's true it's a good thing to not "go off" at people. However, it is plastic compared to the real fruit of His patience He wants to grow in you.

Any one of us can learn human "anger management." However, most human anger is unrighteous anger leading us to thunder against people in our hearts, words, and actions.

You have heard that our ancestors were told, 'You must not murder. If you commit murder, you are subject to judgment.' But I say, if you are even angry with someone, you are subject to judgment! If you call someone an idiot, you are in danger of being brought before the court. And if you curse someone, you are in danger of the fires of hell. Matthew 5:21-22

Jesus doesn't mince words. Just as He says in Matthew 5:28 that lust is adultery in your heart, so here He says that unrighteous anger is murder in your heart. There is a famine of love in the land because our anger pollutes everything around us.

This will ensure that the land where you live will not be polluted, for murder pollutes the land. And no sacrifice except the execution of the murderer can purify the land from murder. Numbers 35:33

What is the status of anger in your heart right now? Is your anger a righteous expression of His love?

The Lord is love. Even His anger is an expression of His love. Righteous anger is His slow deep burn against real sin and evil because He is holy. He knows real sin and evil enslave and kill people in countless little ways every day. God hates that with the purity of His burning love. It's possible that some of your anger is His righteous slow burn. If so, rest in His love and ask Him to give you more of His heart for the person or situation toward which you are angry.

However, it's more likely that your anger burns from the dark fire of pain, unforgiveness, fear, rejection, vengeance, or greed. Welcome to the human race. Take your anger seriously and take it to Jesus. Rest in His love from unrighteous anger.

Remember, He has taken His wrath for your sin upon Himself on the cross. He put Himself in your place and took hell's heat meant for you. Therefore put yourself in His place in His merciful arms. Get rid of your anger instead of managing it. Jesus is not a manager. He is not a supervisor constantly evaluating everyone in anger. He is Lord—constantly valuing everyone in patient love. Come rest from constantly evaluating yourself and everyone else around you and discover how much He values and loves you and everyone else. Come rest from trying to make a good impression on Him or anyone else. Come rest at His throne of grace, His mercy seat.

Let us then with confidence draw near to the throne of grace, that we may receive mercy and find grace to help in time of need. Hebrews 4:16 ESV

And there I will meet with you, and I will speak with you from above the mercy seat, from between the two cherubim which are on the ark of the Testimony, about everything which I will give you in commandment to the children of Israel. Exodus 25:22 ESV

In Exodus, the Lord told Moses to build an ornate golden box to house the ten commandment tablets. It was adorned with a lid with two gold angels facing one another. The space between the angels was called the mercy seat. This is where the Lord's presence came to rest when He spoke with Moses in the tabernacle tent. After Jesus came 1,500 years later to die for our sins and rise from the dead He ascended to heaven and is seated at the right hand of God the Father. Where Jesus sits is the eternal mercy seat!

Are you angry at someone right now? Are you finding it impossible to be kind? Come rest in the mercy seat, come die to your anger in His arms and rise in His loving-kindness.

Try praying this way, *Lord Jesus, you have died for all my sins. Thank you! In the safety of your presence I cry out to You for help. You know the pain and the anger I feel toward this person and situation. Grateful for Your loving-kindness toward me, I now step out of the judgment seat and come rest in Your mercy seat. I let go of my grudge and place it and this person and situation in Your hands. I ask you to bless this person and fix this situation Your way. Anytime this person and situation comes to my mind help me to bless them and come running to your mercy seat. Teach me to stay in Your mercy seat in all my relationships and situations the rest of my life. Now touch my wounded heart and heal me and take my anger away. Amen!*

Nearly everyone around you is constantly evaluating themselves and devaluing everyone else. People may not be aware of it but they need massive doses of real patience. Help end all this. Come to His throne of grace for your sake, stay at His mercy seat for others' sake.

Real friends don't try to impress you, or require you to impress them. Real friends are slow to anger and quick to be patient. That's Jesus. That's you too if you give Him a chance. He knows you've been burned by your anger and others' anger in the past. But His hands are scarred so yours don't have to be charred!

Only the Lord can help you burn with His righteous anger for sin *yet* stay flowing with real patience toward yourself and every other sinner around you. That is the essence of patience—restraining wrath and releasing mercy.

Start praying for a revival of real patience all around you. Let Him make you the first answer to your prayer! Let the real fireworks begin!

KINDNESS

Real Kindness:
Tenderhearted Mercy

Plastic Kindness:
Being Nice

Chapter 17
Unexpected Mercy

Now which of these three would you say was a neighbor to the man who was attacked by bandits?" Jesus asked. The man replied, "The one who showed him mercy." Then Jesus said, "Yes, now go and do the same.

—Luke 10:36-37

She was a beloved and cantankerous retired English teacher in her late eighties. I was the new twenty-two- year-old pastor, extremely "wet behind the ears." Known to locals as "Miss Jack," she was a veritable institution in the small farming community having taught grammar to countless people for several generations. She was precise yet often blunt in her speech, extremely devout yet hilariously irreverent. She let me call her "Ethel." She called me "Dickie Dear."

When I began growing a beard she sent me a birthday card with one dollar and a message—"Dickie Dear, take this and get at least one side of your face shaved." The following Sunday after worship she came through the hand shaking line and I asked her, "Ethel, don't you like my beard?" She paused eyeing me through her old-fashioned spectacles and exclaimed, "Young man, I don't know whether you look more like a monkey or

Jesus!" and sauntered off amidst the disdainful gasps of her few contemporaries and the giggling of her juniors. She was the master of the caustic quip and a true last word artist. She delivered her lines with a stone straight face belied only by an occasional wink and wry smile that appeared and left like a flitting humming bird.

As communion steward she was fastidious about the preparation of the hand pressed table cloths and deliberate about their exact placement. She insisted the only acceptable juice was Welch's Red Grape Juice "because Jesus' blood was red not purple!" I didn't know much in those days, but I knew enough not to argue.

At the Ladies' Aid Christmas party she whipped out a huge school hand bell in the middle of the singing of "Jingle Bells" and rang it with two-handed, determined, straight faced gusto long after our singing had collapsed into belly laughter.

Ethel couldn't see very well and could hear even less. She would make her way to her seat well before worship began and hold the program close for thorough perusal, blinking quickly behind thick lenses. One Sunday morning, I preached my heart out concerning Jesus' story of the Good Samaritan. As we were singing the concluding hymn I was concerned that Ethel was still seated, intently focused on writing something on her program. She then proceeded to carefully tear the program in two as I was giving the final blessing. After worship she walked up to me in the greeting line and said, "Young man you have the potential to be a fine public speaker. However, if that is to occur you must improve your grammar! In the story of the Good Samaritan, the beaten man was not "laying" on the road. He may have been laying sticks upon the road, but he was not "laying on" the road." She then handed me her paper with several verbs properly conjugated—"lay, lie, lain"; "sit, sat, set"; etc. She peered up at me, blinking not winking. I was busted! I attempted a recovery, "Well thank you Ethel, but I usually don't do too badly, do I?" She replied, "I wouldn't know, I only hear your mistakes!" The skewering complete, she wheeled and left me "lying" upon the road of grammatical dust.

Ethel and her grammar lessons are precious in my memory. More important I will never forget her words, "I only hear your mistakes." Ethel was, of course, playing with me. However, her words describe with deadly precision the accusing, condemning spirit of humanity in this love starved world.

It is not lost on me that her playful quip involved Jesus' story of the Good Samaritan. The revered Jewish priest and the honorable Temple assistant were both religious officials with power and connections to help the beaten man left for dead lying upon the road to Jericho. They lacked the one true thing the dying man needed—God's heart of mercy. They could only hear his groans and see his blood as threat, inconvenience, or contamination.

Then the hated Samaritan who is used to hostile territory comes along. He would have expected poor treatment from locals as well as robbers. Most Jews he would pass on the road would feel an obligation to shun him. Jews and Samaritans understood the rules of cold tolerance. They expected to be ignored by one another.

The Samaritan, however, has real kindness for the beaten man. Real kindness is unilaterally given at real risk to meet real need. Fake kindness is self-serving tolerance.

Real kindness is unexpected mercy. It begins with deep rising emotion and ends in action and follow-up. The Good Samaritan ignores his fear and focuses compassionately on the man's need. The Priest and Levite ignore the man and focus on themselves. Those two clear out of the way. The Samaritan cleans out the man's wounds, applies oil to heal, and provides shelter and ongoing care.

The story of the Good Samaritan is not about people mustering their own kindness to overcome prejudice. The story is really about the guy telling the story. Real kindness, including everlasting "follow up" care from the Holy Spirit, comes only from Jesus who died for this world of robbers. The Bible says Christ died for us while we were all still sinners—like a bunch of robbers and religious hypocrites on the fearful road of life.

What unexpected mercy from a guy who shed red blood—not purple—to cleanse our sins! Because of Christ living in me I can live more like Him, and less like a monkey. For on the cross, He was the true last word artist saying, "Father forgive them, they know not what they do." He paid and finished your debt and mine in full. When He looks at you right now, all He sees is your need for His kindness.

Receive Him afresh right now. Let Him cleanse and heal you. Before long, He'll ask you to follow Him back out on the road of robbers and monkeys—for most people see only the mistakes in themselves and others. Most people expect only more calamities and death. What do you see in your future, more people laying heavy burdens upon each other or more people laying their burdens down at the feet of Unexpected Mercy? Aren't you glad He saw you by the roadside…and did not pass by?

Go and do likewise.

Chapter 18
Easy Does It

Since God chose you to be the holy people he loves, you must clothe yourselves with tenderhearted mercy, kindness, humility, gentleness, and patience. Make allowance for each other's faults, and forgive anyone who offends you. Remember, the Lord forgave you, so you must forgive others. Above all, clothe yourselves with love, which binds us all together in perfect harmony. And let the peace that comes from Christ rule in your hearts. For as members of one body you are called to live in peace. And always be thankful.

—Colossians 3:12-14

Mom called the neighbor lady and told her I would be right over. At six years old, it was a long walk of guilt and fear—only two houses away, but it seemed miles. The neighbor lady told my mother she had just learned I had persuaded her five-year-old daughter to play "doctor." I apologized in tears to Mom but that was only the first step. I needed to go apologize to the neighbor and her daughter. I finally arrived at their back porch. She opened the door and asked me to come in. Her daughter stood next to her. It was hard to do but I told them both "I'm sorry!" I hadn't even finished blurting it out when the neighbor mom opened her arms and I ran to her and she held me as I sobbed cleansing tears. Children need real kindness as they deal with their sin nature. It can make all the difference in the world.

I no longer feel the shame and dread *because* I will always remember her arms of mercy. Mercy given *and* received lifts burdens and heals memories. Kindness births deeper trust and propels us forward into the fruit of faithfulness. The neighbor lady's arms of mercy were a doorway to my destiny as a preacher of His open arms of tenderhearted mercy.

But as for me, I am like a green olive tree in the house of God; I trust in the loving kindness of God forever and ever. Psalm 52:8 NASB

The neighbor had many options. She could have pointed her finger and lectured me. I deserved it. Instead, she opened her arms. My mother knew the kind woman to whom she sent me. The neighbor was a loving mother and wife and a hard working nurse at *Mercy* Hospital. She could see my self-condemnation. She didn't need to add to it. She took it easy on me. In lifting her arms she lifted my burden. That is what makes kindness unique among the fruit of the Spirit. As patience is slow to anger and place a burden, kindness is quick to offer mercy and relieve a burden.

The root word for kindness in Galatians 5 in the fruit of the Spirit passage is the same root word Jesus uses to describe His "easy" yoke in Matthew 11:29. When He calls His yoke easy and His burden light, he's not saying that following Him is a breeze. The word for "easy" means "custom fit, will not chafe." Jesus takes His yoke as you follow Him. His yoke, His arm around you, is "kind" to your shoulders. He doesn't press down and jerk you around. He is gentle in guiding you. We don't deserve such kindness, but that's just who He is. Sooner or later, left to ourselves, any one of us in weakness, fear, or anger will try to press down or jerk people around to get our way. Jesus doesn't. Jesus is kind. He eases burdens for anyone who comes to Him.

If people don't come to Him, He remains kindly toward them but He doesn't force people to come to Him. In spite of all He has done for all humanity, people are still free to go to hell and make life a living hell for themselves and others. He doesn't want that and fights to draw people away from sin's path to hell; and sends His followers out to be His arms of mercy to invite them as well. At the end of time every knee will bow to Jesus. His love is *so* kind seeking as many as possible to come into His merciful arms before it is too late.

For God so loved the world, that he gave his only Son, that whoever believes in him should not perish but have eternal life. John 3:16 ESV

Kindness refreshes the church as well. We need to ease each others' burdens, give each other more slack, stop looking for everything that's wrong in the church, and increase celebration of what's right. The Lord wants us to immerse ourselves in His tenderhearted mercy, make allowance for each others' faults, and be quick to forgive remembering how He has forgiven us. The church needs more kindness than programs, more mercy than buildings, more forgiveness than mission statements.

Your love has given me much joy and comfort, my brother, for your kindness has often refreshed the hearts of God's people. Philemon 1:6-8

Kindness is not the "plastic fruit" of tolerance. Tolerance is prized in our culture but actually condones many things God says are wrong and destructive. And behind "tolerance" is thinly veiled, cold, judgmental anger for anyone it deems "intolerant." Kindness does not ignore the sin of a person. Kindness looks deep beneath the sin to the sinner's burdened heart. Kindness is what made Jesus a "friend of sinners." Kindness doesn't take you off the hook. Kindness keeps the hook from digging deeper.

In John 8, Jesus confronts the crafty condemning crowd and sends them away from the woman caught in adultery. He protects her from the heavy rocks they want to throw. He does not condemn her. Neither does he condone her actions. He sets her free and sends her on her way with the words, "Now go and sin no more." Kindness does not execute you for sin, but empowers you to be free of sin. Is there any burden of sin for which you need cleansing and healing in His arms of mercy? I can be harder on myself than the devil when I stumble in sin. Receiving kindness gets you off your back and back on the job for the Lord.

Once, when we were very young parents, we ran out of gas in the middle of nowhere. I felt so stupid for exposing Kim and our children to this stress and vulnerability. I was really doing a number on myself while we talked about what to do. There were no houses in sight and certainly no cell phones! Suddenly a farmer pulled up in his truck. He smiled and simply offered to go get gas for us. Still trying to figure out some way I could do something to get us out of the mess I caused, I offered to go with Him. He smiled and said, "No, you stay here and protect your family. I'll be right back." His kindness and counsel lifted my burden of condemnation and freed me to actually get back to work being a good protector. He came back shortly and would not accept money. It was important for him to give and for me to receive kindness. No doubt he had been in my place before. His gas filled our tank. His kindness filled our hearts and washed away fear and condemnation.

The Lord is helping me learn to stick close to Him, to remember to hold tight to His hand. Now when I stumble, I'm slower to attack myself and quicker to turn to His smiling face and forgiving arms, back following Him. He can do the same for you.

The LORD directs the steps of the godly. He delights in every detail of their lives. Though they stumble, they will never fall, for the LORD holds them by the hand. Psalm 37:23-24

Recently I awoke with my plan for the day but the Lord had His own plan. Before I knew it, He led me and friends of our ministry to pray for people at a public event where all manner of sinful behavior was condoned. There were no other Christian organizations at this event. The Holy Spirit spontaneously sent us in. When I got the phone call, I thought, "Here we go!" As I was driving I felt like the Lord said to me "Son, stay by my thigh." Then I saw a picture in my mind as if I was with Jesus at Grand Central Station in New York in the midst of a massive chaotic crowd and I was a three-year-old boy. He offered His hand and told to me to stick close. I then prayed as we teach others in our ministry,

Dear Jesus, give me Your heart for the people I meet. Help me feel what You feel, help me see what You see, help me know what You know for loving these people Your way. I step out of the judgment seat and rest in Your mercy seat. Help me to love them from Your heart at Your leading. Amen.

When I arrived I felt anxious someone might mistake my motive for being there. I hoped no one from the newspaper took my picture! Suddenly, it was like He tugged on my hand and reassured me. I realized the Holy Spirit's fire was burning fear of man off me. I saw many things that break His heart, especially lots of children and youth being encouraged to believe this was all okay. Yet I experienced an even deeper sense of being a little boy holding Jesus' hand. He yearned for every one there to take His hand! I then began to see beneath the sin to peoples' burdened hearts and started feeling, seeing, and knowing things from His heart. As I walked onto the park grounds He took me back to the night He was born in Bethlehem and I felt like He said, "Just as you are walking into this park, so did I walk into this world of sin in Bethlehem. The world was lost, and I was born. This is My heart." Suddenly, when I looked at people I felt overwhelmed as He showed me the pain, fear, and often angry rage of each wounded heart in each person—every one absolutely precious to Him.

I found my friends who were already praying. They felt the Lord had led them to offer free "spiritual readings" to people. Wow! It sounds crazy, but people started lining up and it continued for three hours! I told my friends about the Lord saying, "Stay by my thigh!" One of them said, "In Revelation 19:16 it says that when Jesus returns upon His thigh will be written, 'King of Kings, Lord of Lords!'" Wow! That told us He did not want us being timid about naming Him to the people. He was okay with giving "spiritual readings" as long as we told them Jesus was the source. He is not afraid or ashamed of being associated with His children and He does not want us to be afraid or ashamed of being associated with Him. The Lord wants us to be mercifully honest. For hours He simply had me ask, "Lord what are their wounds and what is your destiny for them if they put their trust in You?" Wounds, destiny, and invitation—His agenda. He didn't speak of their sin. He didn't want me to go there.

Before I sat down and prayed with the first person at the table, the Lord put Matthew 7:1-5 on my heart. I then looked at the man and felt like the Lord showed me He wanted this man to be His man of wise counsel all the days of his life *if* He would put his trust in the Lord. We did not know each other and he looked at me with surprise and told me he was a middle school counselor. Jesus knew. Two women came up and I felt like the Lord showed me a picture of a little girl pulling a red wagon along in her neighborhood. She was filling her wagon with damaged teddy bears. I felt like the Lord was saying that she had been roughed up and cast aside like those bears but as she came to Jesus' arms, He would heal her and lead her to bring other roughed up people to Him. Her eyes sparkled as she said, "You are talking about Jesus aren't you? I'm born again. He's my Lord and Savior. You know what, my friend needs Jesus as her Savior." At that point her friend started backing up. She wasn't sure she had signed on for all this. I asked her if it was alright if I prayed for her and she said a timid "Yes." It was a small sure beginning of good things for her, too. Real kindness propels His church beyond the four walls every time.

He is very good at convicting people of their sin. We are all very accomplished at condemning ourselves. People don't need you to point out their sin as much as they need your kindness, prayers, testimony, and invitation to come rest in Jesus' arms. It was amazing. At the "spiritual readings" table there was nothing spooky. We were simply praying silently and sharing with people things Jesus was laying upon our hearts for them. Time after time He would show me some wound from their past and some promise of a loving life if they trusted Jesus who loved them *so.*

He released so much love that the organizers invited us to come to a nearby city for their next event. Many once again came to the table, and curiously, as they received such unexpected kindness from Jesus' friends they began to confess and repent of their own sins. No one had to bring it up. Amazing Jesus! Several received Jesus by faith and asked the Holy Spirit to overflow in their lives. Others just needed kindness, prayer, or a listening ear. There was also a poignant moment when we saw other Christians standing on the outside of the event waving placards of protest. The Lord does not want me to unkindly stand in condemnation of those Christians. Yet, I am forever changed by the Friend of Sinners. He may lead you to lift a placard of protest at ungodliness. But please make sure it's not your own sin, fear, shame, anger, or condemnation leading you instead of Him. Both believers and not-yet-believers struggle under way too much condemnation in this famine of love. Jesus more often calls us to be "living letters" of kindness rather than carry placards of protest.

You show that you are a letter from Christ, the result of our ministry, written not with ink but with the Spirit of the living God, not on tablets of stone but on tablets of human hearts. 2 Corinthians 2:3-4 NIV

For a moment now, just sit back and let this same Scripture soak deep into your heart. Here are two different versions. Before you read, close your eyes a moment and ask Jesus to sit next to you and give you more of His heart for people, and yourself, as He speaks to you through this passage.

Do not judge, or you too will be judged. For in the same way you judge others, you will be judged, and with the measure you use, it will be measured to you. Why do you look at the speck of sawdust in your brother's eye and pay no attention to the plank in your own eye? How can you say to your brother, 'Let me take the speck out of your eye,' when all the time there is a plank in your own eye? You hypocrite, first take the plank out of your own eye, and then you will see clearly to remove the speck from your brother's eye. Matthew 7:1-5 NIV

Jesus spoke plain talk to people who were passing sentence on others in their minds. That's what "judging" means, to pass sentence. Only One person has been given authority to pass spiritual sentence on anybody. We can end the famine of love when we let Jesus be the judge and jury. Even in this very tough talk, Jesus expresses kindness through His sense of humor straight out of the carpenter shop. Your sin is like a plank in your eye. It's hilarious and true—it's a plank because only the Kind One can help you get it out. You can't win your own struggle with sin. It's a heavy plank that burdens and blinds you. To Jesus, your sin is like a speck, easy for Him to remove if you will surrender to Him. Once your eye is bathed in His mercy, He will help you see that another's sin is like a speck to Him too. Until they trust Him, your job is to ease their load—not add to it. Let this tough humorous truth Jesus clear your vision of others.

Life is hard enough in this culture of condemnation without making it harder. Come into His Arms and let Him hold you a long time. Rest from being judge and jury. Get off your own back, ride on His back, and ease burdens on others' backs.

Take His hand, stay by His thigh, and invite others to do the same. So many wounded souls are lost in the shuffle at Grand

Central Station. Your real kindness can usher them safely through the crowd. Who is it that has been roughed up and cast aside? Who is it that desperately needs His kindness through you?

End the famine of love. Easy does it.

So get rid of all evil behavior. Be done with all deceit, hypocrisy, jealousy, and all unkind speech. Like newborn babies, you must crave pure spiritual milk so that you will grow into a full experience of salvation. Cry out for this nourishment, now that you have had a taste of the Lord's kindness. 1 Peter 2:1-3

Let's pray:

Dear Jesus, give me Your heart for the people I meet. Help me feel what You feel, help me see what You see, help me know what You know for loving these people Your way. I step out of the judgment seat and rest in Your mercy seat. Help me to love them from Your heart at Your leading. Amen.

Chapter 19

Healing Hands, Warm Heart

As soon as Jesus heard the news, he left in a boat to a remote area to be alone. But the crowds heard where he was headed and followed on foot from many towns. Jesus saw the huge crowd as he stepped from the boat, and he had compassion on them and healed their sick.

—Mark 14:13-15

I heard it countless times, “Cold hands, warm heart!” For years, after worship I shook hands with parishioners and was embarrassed at cold hands. At all other times my hands were warm as oven mitts. This was performance anxiety. The Lord showed me that I was sometimes fearfully striving to “do a good job” rather than resting in Him as I was preaching His good news. The Lord has delivered me of this fear and helped me unlearn old ways. Once in a great while I still slip back into this fear when preaching or leading an event but now the occasional cold hands are simply a reminder to “rest on His chest.”

Real kindness is not fearful striving to help people. Real kindness is resting in the Father’s compassion and reaching out to heal others in some way. That's who Jesus was, that's who Jesus *is*.

It's safe to assume Jesus never had cold hands from anxiety because there is no Scripture where it says He was afraid. He constantly chose to rest in His Father's bosom. That's why the devil and people were never able to manipulate Him. "Manipulate" means to twist with the hands. No one could twist Jesus because His hands were always healing hands connected to the Father's compassionate heart. He was pure unbounded compassion on the loose, wanting everyone who came to Him to be healed in every way. He feared no one, He loved everyone. People often forget that it was Jesus Himself speaking these famous words to Nicodemus one night.

For God did not send His Son into the world to condemn the world, but that the world through Him might be saved. John 3:17 NKJV

Even when Jesus was calling Herod a "fox" or the Pharisees "hypocrites" He loved them by truthfully calling them out. From the cross He prayed the kindest words ever spoken "Father forgive them, they know not what they do." After He died, the compassionate Father raised Him so all who call upon Jesus can experience His healing compassion.

A few years ago I had the delight of making acquaintance with Ted Neeley, the original star of the 1970s rock opera "Jesus Christ Superstar." Ted was a rock drummer serendipitously cast in the role of Jesus. "Superstar" was a huge play, movie, and soundtrack criticized by many as sacrilegious. It was written by Andrew Lloyd Webber who was not a believer. Webber's story ends in an anticlimactic scene with no mention of Jesus rising from the dead. However, when Ted Neeley agreed to reprise the role of Jesus for a twenty-fifth anniversary tour of the show, he insisted that a condition of his return be the show depict Jesus rising from the dead. The Lord had won Ted over through the role and he eventually gave His life to Jesus. As he got to know the Living Jesus he welcomed the chance to honor Jesus the second time around!

My favorite part of Ted Neeley's reprise of "Superstar" came when He would reenact the scene from Mark 14. As Jesus (Neely) was attempting to draw apart with his disciples to a secluded place for rest and renewal, the clamoring desperate crowds caught up with him. At one point Ted almost violently pauses in agony and then compassionately flings himself back toward the crowd laying healing hands on every one of them. I will never forget it. A play actor's mannerism perfectly capturing the heart of a Savior who in real life had compassionately captured him! I thanked Ted for that depiction after the play and he celebrated that I noticed, because that was his moment of personal tribute to his compassionate Lord.

Over the years we have seen the Living Lord miraculously heal a variety of life threatening illnesses. The first miraculous healing I witnessed was my cousin who was my childhood best friend. In the early '90s, she was a young wife and mother when she was diagnosed with dozens of "incurable" cancerous tumors throughout the organs of her body. Many around her gave her no chance to live. She was challenged by a psychiatrist to stop being "in denial" and get her affairs in order and to tell her young children she was going to die. She refused to receive such defeatist "death thinking" in her mind and heart and instead placed her complete trust in Jesus for healing and guidance. She received by faith the healing prayers of His people and the Holy

Spirit's guidance on what medical and alternative treatments to receive. After receiving healing prayer from a Catholic priest known for healing ministry, she felt in her spirit that Jesus had healed her. She refused any prognosis of her future that did not include complete recovery. Her trust gave the Lord, and herself, real opportunity for healing and miracle. She trusted the Lord's faithfulness and compassion for herself and her family. She not only believed He could heal her, but she believed He *would* heal her. That is true faith. A few months later, the doctors were stunned and we were all ecstatic to discover that her body scans showed every tumor was gone. Now, twenty years later, she just graduated from law school and continues to live into the Lord's purposes for her life. Please remember to always accept Christ and never accept death no matter what people tell you. Death is not God's friend, death is not your friend, Jesus is your Friend.

For he must reign until he has put all his enemies under his feet. The last enemy to be destroyed is death. 1 Corinthians 15:25-26 ESV

Do not fear death and yet do not befriend it. Death is the product of sin. Christ's victory over death is the seed of the fruit of the Spirit.

For the sin of this one man, Adam, caused death to rule over many. But even greater is God's wonderful grace and his gift of righteousness, for all who receive it will live in triumph over sin and death through this one man, Jesus Christ. Romans 5:17

With Jesus, you never have to fear or dread death. He will be with you all the way through it. Doctors and medicine can be a blessing from the Lord for diagnosis and treatment, but never prognosis. Let no man tell you that you are incurable or "terminal." To agree that your illness is unto death can actually block your healing and is an expression of unbelief. Jesus has not only given us victory over death, He has also given His true followers authority over all disease.

One day Jesus called together his twelve disciples and gave them power and authority to cast out all demons and to heal all diseases. Luke 9:1

A slightly cynical person once asked me, "Does everyone you pray for get healed?" I replied, "Not yet." Anytime someone is not healed is all the more reason to keep praying for healing. Because the biggest reason to pray for healing is to honor Jesus and give His compassion opportunity to move in our midst.

Praise the LORD, my soul, and forget not all his benefits— who forgives all your sins and heals all your diseases, who redeems your life from the pit and crowns you with love and compassion. Psalm 103:2-4 NIV

Jesus' hands are kind hands. From the Lord's perspective, all healings are an expression of His kindness. His kindness comes deep from His heart, deep from His guts. No matter how much He needed to draw apart and rest, when the hurting crowds tracked Him down, He would turn and heal them all.

By witnessing healings and miracles, I have learned the Lord moves with compassion in response to faith, praise, and thanksgiving for who Christ is and all He has done on the cross.

At a Benny Hinn crusade, I witnessed Benny's tenderhearted kindness for the sick and infirm of all ages. His simple proclamation of Jesus' death and resurrection, together with sustained worship which focused us all in praise and thanksgiving to Jesus for the cross, brought healing to many. As thousands sang with all their hearts, hundreds came forward to testify to their healings. Benny laid hands on very few people but the presence of Jesus, through the Holy Spirit, touched many.

From Benny I learned that when we stop focusing on our illnesses and pour ourselves out upon Jesus, our Heavenly Father is so pleased and proud of His Son's sacrifice, that He dispatches the Holy Spirit to release signs and wonders on a broad scale. Real preaching of the gospel is simple spoken praise and thanksgiving for what Jesus has done on the cross and inviting people to reap all His benefits. This is happening all over the earth, anywhere Jesus is lifted up *and* allowed to do miracles. It's been that way for over 2,000 years. Yet, many are in true denial of His available power.

And because of their unbelief, he couldn't do any miracles among them except to place his hands on a few sick people and heal them. And he was amazed at their unbelief. Mark 6:5-6

The reason we see so few healings and miracles today is not because the Lord no longer does them. It's because His people generally do not allow Him to do all He can for them. It's just the way the Lord is. He waits in compassion for those who have real faith in Him. If we trust Him for healing, praising all His benefits of the cross for our forgiveness of sins *and* the healing of our diseases then He responds with signs and wonders. Try it.

The problem of unbelief, doubt, or cynicism is rooted in fear. There is a little boy or girl inside each of us that desperately wants to be loved and accepted. Therefore we each have some measure of fear of rejection, abandonment, or aloneness. I have seen it in others and in myself. We won't quite risk asking and trusting Jesus to heal us because we fear if it doesn't happen it might mean He does not love us or we are not worthy. But the Lord has decided we are all worth it.

A man with leprosy came and knelt in front of Jesus, begging to be healed. "If you are willing, you can heal me and make me clean," he said. Moved with compassion, Jesus reached out and touched him. "I am willing," he said. "Be healed!" Instantly the leprosy disappeared, and the man was healed. Matthew 1:40-42

The Lord is always willing to heal you. Sometimes He is aiming for a deeper healing first. We once prayed for a woman who was told she had terminal cancer. As we prayed the Lord showed her He wanted her to let go of a grudge she had carried for sixty years. She let the grudge go to the Lord and forgave that person in her heart. We then prayed for the disease to go and she was healed. For all we know, she was healed the moment she trusted Jesus would heal her and let go of the grudge.

I tell you the truth, you can say to this mountain, 'May you be lifted up and thrown into the sea,' and it will happen. But you must really believe it will happen and have no doubt in your heart. I tell you, you can pray for anything, and if you believe that you've received it, it will be yours. But when you are praying, first forgive anyone you are holding a grudge against, so that your Father in heaven will forgive your sins, too. Mark 11:22-25

Doubt, unforgiveness, and other unrepentant sin are blocks to healing and the miraculous move of the Spirit. If we trust our compassionate Jesus to live His childlike way, then we will be healed and become living vessels of his healing for others. The more that I come rest from doubt, fear, unforgiveness, and other unrepentant sin, the more I have been filled by the Lord's compassion and faith and seen healings and miracles in response to my prayers.

Sometimes we are so "comfortably miserable" in our circumstance or have resigned ourselves to poor health that we don't want to be healed nor can we imagine it. If you don't want to be healed He won't force it on you.

One man was there who had been an invalid for thirty-eight years. When Jesus saw him lying there and knew that he had already been there a long time, he said to him, "Do you want to be healed?" John 5:5-6 ESV

The Lord wants to heal everyone physically, emotionally, spiritually, relationally—because He is kind. If you want Him to grow His fruit of real kindness in you, then let the arm of the Lord move through your life!

Awake, awake, put on strength, O arm of the LORD; awake, as in days of old, the generations of long ago. Was it not you who cut Rahab in pieces, who pierced the dragon? Isaiah 51:9 ESV

In the early Methodist awakening in England in the middle 1700s John Wesley would cry out in prayer at gatherings, "Arm of the Lord, awake!" Faith would rise, demons would flee, healings and miracles were released, and people would receive a new song of joy in their mouths. The Arm of the Lord is what set Israel free from Pharaoh. The Arm of the Lord is the Holy Spirit releasing His merciful gifts to destroy the works of the enemy. Real kindness from Jesus destroys real evil with real power.

The Arm of the Lord moves like this: ask the Holy Spirit to release more of His gift of faith in you for believing declaration of healing and miracle. At the first declaration of faith for healing, the recovery begins but may not be complete for a while. Do not despair, or let others be discouraged. Healing means progressive recovery and takes place over whatever measure of time the Lord determines. But miracle is instantaneous. There are healing miracles but also other supernatural instant reversals of natural conditions. Faith, healing, and miracles are not things you muster, but gifts of kindness you invite and declare with the Lord. The question is will we believe, forgive, and declare His praise? Pause a moment and let the following words sink in deeply.

Who has believed what he has heard from us? And to whom has the arm of the LORD been revealed? But he was wounded for our transgressions; he was crushed for our iniquities; upon him was the chastisement that brought us peace, and with his stripes we are healed. Isaiah 53:1, 5 ESV

Many years ago, during Sunday praise singing, I asked the Lord what He wanted to do that morning. In my heart I heard him say, "I want to heal someone's right shoulder. I want to heal someone's left knee. I want to heal someone's liver, specifically at the bile duct." It was one of the first times I felt led to call out something that specific to the congregation. I felt a little nervous because I knew that some believed and others did not. I announced what I felt I heard the Lord say and encouraged anyone with those problems to trust the Lord for healing and to let someone pray in agreement with them after service. Afterward a family I had never met walked up to me. It was a mother, father and two teenage daughters. The mother said, "This is the first time we have ever been here and I don't quite know what to make of it, but I am the person with the right shoulder problem." I said, "Praise the Lord! Let's pray!" She said, "Yes, but also I'm the person with the left knee problem." I proclaimed, "Awesome! Let's pray!" She persisted, "You need to know also that two months ago surgeons opened me up and visibly inspected an inoperable massive growth on my liver located at the bile duct. They tell me there is nothing they can do. Mayo Clinic supposedly has an experimental life threatening procedure and this week I'm to go up to be tested to see if I qualify for them to even try it." The whole family had tears in their eyes. So did I. We joined hands and prayed.

After the testing she waited to be summoned for surgery. Instead, a simple letter arrived from Mayo's pathology department informing her, "No tumor present. Healthy liver. No follow up necessary." Thank you Jesus. When the mother gave her testimony in church, she told everyone that when I prayed with the family she heard me say, "God says it's going to be okay." She held on to that word with faith, much like so many of the sick in the Bible held onto Jesus' garment. I don't remember saying that to her, but I'm sure the Lord said it to her. He lives. So does that mother. Later that summer one of the daughters went on our youth mission trip and received Jesus as her Lord and Savior. That is the ultimate healing the Lord was aiming at when He healed her mother.

And wherever he came, in villages, cities, or countryside, they laid the sick in the marketplaces and implored him that they might touch even the fringe of his garment. And as many as touched it were made well. Mark 6:56 ESV

Recently, a woman came to us for prayer on behalf of her not-yet-saved friend and co-worker. She stood by faith and asked us to lay hands on her and pray healing for her friend's pancreatic cancer. She then called her friend and told her we three had prayed. The co-worker then went to the Mayo Clinic the next week and was told her cancer was gone. Our friend was the first person she called.

We have a fifty-year-old friend who fought a ten-year-long battle with cancer. One day, we were informed her health was failing and she was at Hospice. Hospice has many caring people who have compassion for those who are dying and for their families. The problem is that everything is predicated on helping a person die in an atmosphere of love. That's the best the world has to offer. But the Lord has much more. The first time we visited our friend, she did indeed seem very near death. Though some friends still were praying for a miracle, others felt her time was short and it might be time to say goodbye. Kim and I went to her and asked the Holy Spirit to come. We then simply asked for healing then commanded healing and miracle in Jesus' name. We encouraged her husband to not give up, but look up. As we left we both felt a deep righteous anger well up within us which we realized was from the Lord. He has righteous anger mixed in with His compassion for people. He hates anything that torments people. As we drove away we felt Him leading us to pray that this illness would not stand. We prayed against a spirit of unbelief and death and declared by faith that she would not die prematurely and that nothing but the arm of the Lord would take her out of this life. As we prayed a picture began forming in my mind. I saw that four or five days hence she would awaken out of this near death experience and great glory would be given to Jesus and overwhelming fire of the Spirit would sweep her family, friends, and church. Five days later we received a call from her husband to tell us she came out of it and knew everyone, was of good cheer, and was beginning to take food. Praise the Lord. Our friend and her husband joyfully received our regular visits and prayers based upon our faith that Jesus wanted to heal her. The Lord told us to honor Him with bold prayers in which we asked and declared her healing in His name. Jesus says to both ask the Father for whatever we will, and to command healing in His authority. Each time we visited she rallied and there was dramatic evidence of improvement. It was a battle, but the Lord told us all to persevere. He had a great purpose in all of it. The Bible tells us that the Lord alone determines the days of our lives. But it is possible to go prematurely. Why else did He give us authority over diseases unless to heal and forestall death for His purposes. Our friend was weak and weary, but we were to be like those who cut a hole in the roof and lowered their paralyzed friend down to Jesus long ago. Jesus saw their faith and healed their friend. The Lord moved in each of our repeated visits to bring love and improvement over the next two months. During this time, our friend was released from the Hospice house because her condition no longer fit with their purpose! She wasn't dying, she was recovering against all odds and medical prognosis. Praise the Lord! Our friend and her husband enjoyed three rich months of increasing health, unprecedented sweetness in their marriage, deep emotional healing of old wounds, and many opportunities to testify to the Lord's miraculous love. Then, suddenly, she died and we were all left to consider what this meant. Quite honestly, I don't understand it all and know it is of no profit to grasp for a pat answer. Her husband, though grieving and missing her, continues to joyfully testify to the Lord's kindness for giving them three more months of richness no one believed possible and no one can ever take away from them.

I am learning to rest on Jesus' chest and resist the temptation to theologize about such things. All I know is that as long as we have breath we are to praise Jesus and declare His healing kindness with deep faith. One thing is for sure, her husband

and I will never forget how the Holy Spirit both inspired and responded to our prayers which were foolish in man's eyes and faithful in the Lord's eyes.

That brings me to my twelve-year-old friend who at age ten became paralyzed from the waist down when a surgery went wrong. It has been difficult and painful for both him and his parents. Many of us are contending for His miraculous healing. When I visited him in the hospital following the paralysis, I felt like the Lord spoke to my heart, "Tell him to ask Me to heal Him, trust Me to heal Him, and work with Me to heal him." We keep asking the Lord to release more of His gifts of faith, healing, and miracles in Seth and in us. In prayer one day the Lord showed me a picture of a palm tree. I reported this to Seth's dad who then found Project Walk on the internet—an organization which is pioneering restorative exercises for spinal injury patients. Most of the medical establishment has no faith for complete recovery once the spinal cord is injured "beyond repair." Not the people of Project Walk. Though they are not explicitly a Christian organization, they believe a person will recover with the right attitude, help, and exercise. By the way, their logo is a palm tree! The Lord's arm is at work in all this. Seth, his family, and friends are asking Jesus, trusting Jesus, and working with Jesus for his healing.

The Lord calls His people to follow His lead and boldly go where fear will not. Real kindness is bold and never gives up or settles for anything less than God's best.

There was once a day that my timid heart did not believe the truths I have written in this chapter. If you find yourself like I once was, then simply, deeply, sincerely ask the Lord to release

His gifts of faith, healing, and miracles in you. Keep asking, keep trusting, keep working with Him.

In the famine of love, people need truly kind friends who really believe Jesus still saves, heals, and delivers. Here is a set of prayer declarations of faith, based on the Scriptures, which you can use for any illness. Share these and pray these for others and yourself as you take authority in Christ over all infirmity, big or small!

The Arm of the Lord is just waiting for you to give Him a chance.

Lord Jesus, I now come rest in Your love.

I renounce all doubt, grudges, and unrepentant sin. (Confess these and give them to the Lord.)

Arm of the Lord awake over me.

Holy Spirit please release the gift of faith, healing, and miracles within me to overflowing.

Lord Jesus, I want you to heal me.

Lord Jesus, I trust you to heal me.

Lord Jesus, help me work with You to heal me.

Father, in the name of Jesus, by the power of His precious blood I now command a spirit of doubt, a spirit of infirmity, and a spirit of death and destruction to leave me now.

I command every cell of my body to be healed in Jesus' name, with the power of His blood.

Lord Jesus, I now declare that by Your stripes I am healed.

In the name of Jesus, with the power of His precious blood, I now declare full recovery and long fruitful life for myself and my family, in body, soul and spirit.

Come Holy Spirit, lead me forward this day to boldly proclaim Jesus' love in my words, prayers, and deeds.

Amen.

GOODNESS

Real Goodness:
Radical Generosity

Plastic Goodness:
Moral Correctness

Chapter 20

Free Stuff!

Heal the sick, cleanse the lepers, raise the dead, cast out demons. Freely you have received, freely give.

—Matthew 10:8 NKJV

You must each decide in your heart how much to give. And don't give reluctantly or in response to pressure. "For God loves a person who gives cheerfully" And God will generously provide all you need. Then you will always have everything you need and plenty left over to share with others. As the Scriptures say, "They share freely and give generously to the poor. Their good deeds will be remembered forever."

—2 Corinthians 9:7-9

My wife Kim and I recently celebrated our thirty-first anniversary of marriage. Though she is a trained secondary school teacher, she lives her life more as a "primary truths" teacher. She sees and shares simple lessons in life, nature, and relationships. She has taught me so much. For example, she decided long ago to never pass a child's lemonade stand and invited me to do the same. I have learned life goes too fast not to!

One day we drove upon what we presumed was a lemonade stand. Five young girls were jumping up and down in their front yard with placards shouting for us to stop. They need not have worried.

We rolled our window down and they all leaned in shrieking, "Free stuff! Free stuff! Free stuff!" We waited a moment for them to calm down and Kim gently protested, "No girls, really, how much is the lemonade? We're happy to pay." To which the littlest girl bubbled, "No, no, no, we have all the money we need! We are giving away free stuff! It's all free!"

More jumping and shrieking! The littlest one held out a shiny necklace of green beads and asked breathlessly, "Would you like it?" Kim could barely stop giggling enough to take it and say, "Okay, thank you so much!" Even more jumping, shrieking, and a chorus of "You're welcome!" as they took off running for their front door to tell Mom.

Have you ever giggled in awe? We couldn't stop! Then we grew still, relishing this snapshot of Jesus' real goodness, His radical generosity, His real church.

Real giving isn't selling for a price. Real giving isn't buying influence or affection. Real giving isn't seeking a desired response or even a "thank you." That's manipulation—looks good on the surface, but phony underneath. Real giving of your time, talents, and treasure has no strings attached. God loves a "cheer-ful" giver. Real giving comes from a heart full of cheer. The Bible word for "cheerful" is the same root word for "hilarious"!

Every time we think of those girls and the green beads it is *very* hilarious!

The world's definition of "goodness" means "moral correctness." This is more plastic fruit. Looks good, sounds good, but is *not good.* The real fruit of the Holy Spirit called "goodness" means "radical hilarious generosity." When you finally *decide* Jesus is all you need and *trust* He will take care of you—that's when the Holy Spirit begins to explode real goodness from deep within you!

To be full of cheer means "joyfully ready." As you rejoice with the Holy Spirit that Jesus saved you, joy for your salvation will always move you to *be good*—ready to give freely. Do you see again how one fruit is precedent to another? Real joy is your real motivation for real goodness. You are joyfully free of fear and joyfully free to give as much as the Holy Spirit leads. Remember, the Lord says don't give reluctantly or begrudgingly. That's not giving. That's not goodness. That's plastic correctness.

Also, the Lord says don't give under pressure because something or someone says you *should.* The longer I live with the Lord the more suspicious I am of plastic "shoulds" and "have to's".

You are now free to trust and obey every command in the Bible in the Spirit's power. You are also free in Jesus to disregard all pressure from the world, or your own flesh, to share what He has given you. Beware of "religious" reasons, but cue into "relationship" promptings from the Lord.

If you ask Him to lead you through each day and give you opportunities to give—He will! When the opportunity arises in some conversation or situation He will remind you of your free gift of salvation and prompt you to give from your glad heart and empty your hands. Remember, you don't *have to* give—you *get* to! And deep down you will feel His pleasure big time.

He also says don't give conditionally with one hand expecting to receive back with your other hand. You don't give in hopes of receiving something because, like our little friend with the green beads, you already have all you need—Him! His bonus promise is that when He sees you truly giving with joyful generosity, He will bring more resources to you to give away. He abhors hoarding and generates generosity. So no worries!

When he arrived and saw this evidence of God's blessing, he was filled with joy, and he encouraged the believers to stay true to the Lord. Barnabas was a good man, full of the Holy Spirit and strong in faith. And many people were brought to the Lord. Acts 11:23-24

There is a famine of real goodness because of two main reasons: we have fearfully forgotten the Lord *is* GOOD; and we have fearfully refused to let the Lord generate goodness in us. Barnabas was a good man, full of the Holy Spirit, and full of faith. All three realities go hand in hand. You cannot be good (radically joyfully generous) if you are not full to overflowing with the personal presence of the Holy Spirit. You cannot be full of the Holy Spirit until You fully trust the Lord Jesus to be your everything.

How about you? Are you good, full of the Holy Spirit, and full of faith in Jesus? If so, celebrate! It's His desired destiny for you. It's guaranteed to everybody who keeps surrendering to Jesus. If you're not there yet, give Him your trust and ask Him for more of the generous Holy Spirit and more opportunities to be his generous child.

Try this on for size right now. Practice saying aloud, "I am a good child of the Father, full of the Holy Spirit, and full of faith!" Maybe you are not quite there yet, but such a positive declaration over yourself is an act of real faith that will trigger an explosion of goodness within your spirit. The Holy Spirit will be right there helping you make the necessary adjustments.

Look at Barnabas. He was as flawed as you and I. The Holy Spirit is the same. Many people came to the Lord around Barnabas. He was always ending a famine of love! Barnabas' name meant "son of encouragement." He knew he was an adopted son of the Father because Jesus had radically and generously saved Him. He radically opened himself to be filled with the Holy Spirit. He trusted the Lord as His provider. He became living encouragement wherever he went.

He was truly a man of the second chance. Barnabas and Paul ministered far and wide. They were powerful partners in the spread of the good news of Jesus. Paul then had a conflict with another co-worker named John Mark. Paul apparently no longer trusted John Mark and refused to work with him. However, Barnabas generously offered to make room for John Mark. He gave him a second chance. This must have been life giving. Paul and Barnabas both saw the wisdom in this and parted ways in their ongoing mission. Certainly Paul bore much fruit in his life, but goodness always shined in Barnabas.

Who around you who needs a second chance?

So many people around you only believe they get what they pay for when Jesus is offering all that He paid for. I want to be like Barnabas the rest of my life! I want to be truly hilarious wherever Jesus leads—just like that little girl with sparkling green beads calling, "Free stuff! Free stuff!"

How about you? Giggling awe awaits.

Let us pray.

Lord, you are hilarious! Make me hilarious too! I want to become your good child, full of the Holy Spirit, and full of faith in You. I now cut all the strings of fearful selfishness. Lead me to freely give as You have freely given to me. In Jesus' name, with the power of His precious blood. Amen.

Chapter 21

Pause and Wonder

But Mary kept all these things and pondered them in her heart.

—Luke 2:19 NKJV

Then He went down with them and came to Nazareth, and was subject to them, but His mother kept all these things in her heart.

—Luke 2:51 NKJV

Mary pondered everything, both at Jesus' birth and when he was twelve… all the time. She declared herself the Lord's handmaiden, totally willing to pause and wonder. That typifies the lifestyle of love Jesus offers. Consider this word play equation; **pause + wonder = ponder.**

When life is too fast, too slow, too heavy, too sad, too intense—it's just the right time to pause and wonder. Look around... look within... pause and wonder at what He has done for you and me and the whole world.

Your attitude should be the same that Christ Jesus had. Though he was God, he did not demand and cling to his rights as God. He laid aside his mighty power and glory and was born in the likeness of men and was found in appearance as a man. Philippians 2:5

Ponder that… pause and wonder... at the radical generosity... before the first Christmas, Christ had unlimited power and freedom of movement...

…John 1 says He was present in the beginning and everything was made through Him.

The Father so loved the world that He asked His eternal Son to give up the unlimited life He knew and submit to become a single cell, to grow as a vulnerable child for nine months in Mary's womb…

....to be born in a feeding trough for animals; honored by shepherds many considered to be riff-raff; to parents who had to flee with him, a babe in arms, to Egypt in order to protect Him from horrible King Herod... to grow up in the disreputable town of Nazareth... a twelve-year-old who amazed the religious teachers in the temple with his questions... and Mary pondered often—preparing for a day she might have hoped could someday be avoided—when the son of her womb would take lashes on his back for our healing and nails in his hands and feet for our sins and would actually die—cease to exist—as dead as a doornail—that receiving him we might have everlasting life.

Ponder that.

....pause and wonder... at the radical generosity of the Maker who hung on a Cross for you... pause and wonder at the radical generosity of beautiful snowflakes, the color and texture of every person's skin, hair, eyes, the timbre of each unique voice in a shopping mall...

…pause and wonder at every evidence of true radical generosity—it is simply an echo of the beautiful voice who once said, "I lay my life down of my own accord, no one takes my life from me. I have come that you would have life and life abundant!"

As I paused and wondered the other day, I thought of Mabel who was a deeply faithful, spritely, feisty, retired science teacher in her '80s. She was a scientist of the heart. She observed and tuned into the exact details of your personality and let you know she loved you as you were. She had open arms for people of all ages and stations in life. Mabel always let my toddler son Daniel run into her arms and picked him up even though he was the most solid kid in history. I remember her joy that he would always come running to her for a hug and her laughter as she squeezed him saying, "I love you, Daniel!" When he grew a bit bigger, his mamma watched in horror as he ran headlong into her waiting arms and knocked her flat on the floor! The ever loving Mabel just picked herself up from the floor laughing and finished the hug!

Mabel was a wonderful mixture of intimate acceptance and dignified formality. She insisted on calling me Richard though most people called me Dick, yet became my dear friend, confidant, and ally in a large church I once served. As I pause and wonder at the gift of Mabel, she was like a combination of my first grade teacher who insisted on calling me Richard and my beloved grandmother who treasured me as her Dickie Boy. It is so *good* to pause and wonder at the richness of God's precious gifts of the particular people He brings into our lives. Before you read further, pause a moment yourself, and ponder the gift of someone special in your life.

Then I pause and wonder at Mabel years later. She sent our ten-year-old daughter Emily flowers after Emily was painfully injured in a serious bike accident. Generous… yes… radically generous… since at that time Mabel lay dying in the hospital...

…radical, radical echoes...

.....of His voice that is speaking to you right now. "I love you, I bless you, I keep you, My face shines upon you, I am always gracious to you. I am lifting up the light of my countenance upon you right now, I give you peace. I love you always, no matter what."

In pausing and wondering the other day, it occurred to me—Jesus never celebrated Christmas, He is Christmas, He is everything!

He wants to be your everything... so, pause and wonder at how big His radical love for you is compared to everything you may fear, everything you may fail in life... and receive Him, deeply, radically….

…then, in light of his Awesome love... everything you see has something to do with Him... it's either a good thing from Him or a bad thing He wants to turn around for your good.

One way or the other, if you pause and wonder, you can see that your life is really His life moving in yours.

The Lord has never failed me with His generous love—and He will never fail you. Trust him… pause and wonder… often.

Then He will be radically generous *through* you…

…pause…

Chapter 22

I Am Not Enough

Day by day the Lord takes care of the innocent, and they will receive an inheritance that lasts forever. They will not be disgraced in hard times; even in famine they will have more than enough.

—Psalm 37:18-19

One sunny day in May many believers in our city gathered at a downtown park for a National Day of Prayer gathering. We had just finished a powerful time of repentance as followers of Christ. Instead of pointing fingers at other sinners in America we lifted our hands and opened our hearts and mouths in confession. We confessed we had failed to love one another and had failed to reflect Jesus and His love to the rest of America.

Your love for one another will prove to the world that you are my disciples. John 13:35

We Christians might fall on our knees before the Lord each Sunday, but we don't stay on our knees serving one another in love Monday through Saturday. Not-yet believers are not attracted to a Jesus whose followers are not growing in real goodness.

Then if my people who are called by my name will humble themselves and pray and seek my face and turn from their wicked ways, I will hear from heaven and will forgive their sins and restore their land. 2 Chronicles 7:14

The Lord is waiting for us who claim His name and blood covering to *truly* humble ourselves, *truly* turn from our sin, and *truly* seek only after Him as a lifestyle. If we do this, He promises to hear our prayers, forgive us, and heal our land. The Lord is looking for our nation to repent, but first He is looking for His people to repent—then He will bless our nation. Let's stop pointing fingers at others' godlessness and start pointing our own lives toward Christlikeness.

As the last praise song finished and the crowd began to disperse I got on my face in the grass before the Lord. For me the repenting had just begun.

I felt like the Lord spoke these pleading words to my heart, "Lately, in all your pain, fear, and anger you have been running everywhere but to me." Then the tone of His voice turned firm and convicting, "I am not enough for you." I began to weep. He continued, "To feel secure you need to see certain results in your loved ones' lives. To feel secure you need to see certain results in your ministry. I am not enough for you." It was very painful. It was very true. It was mercifully liberating.

I didn't realize just how much I was struggling. Sometimes we get so preoccupied about what's not going well that we make our lives the center of our lives. It doesn't work!

Face down in the grass I found, once again, the forgiving face of Real Love. Suddenly I was no longer a "gloomy Gus." I was set free from fear and realized the Lord was *for* my loved ones and *for* me! I was now free to be *for* them, *for* me, in my heart! I instantly began praying *for* my loved ones, not *about* them. Both burden and blinders were lifted. It was a profound moment of deliverance that continues to be a lens through which I look at life, and learn. The Lord is so good.

The New Testament word for goodness means the kind of radical generosity that includes telling you the truth you need, but at the moment may not want! Radical generosity means you are "all in" much more than in the game Texas Hold'em. You are absolutely committed to a person's welfare, regardless of how they respond to you in the moment.

We all need a person or two in our life who are so deeply and permanently committed to us they will risk the flak of our wrath to tell us the truth. They will do it with kindness to be sure, but it may still sting. Sometimes so does the Father's love. There will be people in your life who need goodness from you in the days ahead. No one can be a good parent, good coach, good teacher, or a good friend who is absolutely permissive.

What a loving Father, who would not permit the world to go unhindered on the highway to hell! He sent His Son to bring course correction, to speak the truth in love, to *be* the Truth in Love. Sometimes He wants to send his correcting love to us through others. Will we receive and recognize it as a good gift? Sometimes He wants to send his correcting love to others through us. Will we give it from a heart deeply committed to them?

"I am not enough" now has double meaning and richness. Slowly, but surely He is growing me more content in two things—I am not enough *and* He is. It's changing the way I look at people, ministry, and world events.

Is the Lord enough for you? Until He is enough, nothing else ever will be. Let these words sink in.

Because of the extravagance of those revelations, and so I wouldn't get a big head, I was given the gift of a handicap to keep me in constant touch with my limitations. Satan's angel did his best to get me down; what he in fact did was push me to my knees. No danger then of walking around high and mighty! At first I didn't think of it as a gift, and begged God to remove it. Three times I did that, and then he told me, "My grace is enough; it's all you need. My strength comes into its own in your weakness." Once I heard that, I was glad to let it happen. I quit focusing on the handicap and began appreciating the gift. It was a case of Christ's strength moving in on my weakness. Now I take limitations in stride, and with good cheer, these limitations that cut me down to size—abuse, accidents, opposition, bad breaks. I just let Christ take over! And so the weaker I get, the stronger I become. 2 Corinthians 12:8-10, The Message

Once He is enough *for* you, His goodness will explode *from* you.

Then every trial of yours becomes His adventure.

Then every time you fall short becomes His time to shine.

Be weak in Him so you can be strong for others.

Let's pray:

(If you're a parent or grandparent and ever feel powerless to help your children or grandchildren, remember you forever have great authority in the Lord to pray boldly into the spiritual realm over their lives and destinies. I learned this prayer from Betty Friedzon of King of Kings Church of Buenos Aires, Argentina.

She testified the Holy Spirit taught her this declaration to pray over her children. Kim and I have passed this on to scores of parents and grandparents. Pass it on!)

*"Father, in the name of Jesus, with the power of His precious blood, I call forth (*child's name) *into a future where (*child's name*) is totally ablaze with the love of Christ and living only for the Glory of God. Amen!"*

FAITHFULNESS

Real Faithfulness:
Confident Trust in Him

Plastic Faithfulness:
Determined Self-confidence

Chapter 23

Trust Walking

This is what the Sovereign Lord, the Holy One of Israel, says: "Only in returning to me and resting in me will you be saved. In quietness and confidence is your strength. But you would have none of it."

—Isaiah 30:15

I write this on a day when newscasts clamor of regime change in Egypt. Many fear how this will affect Egypt's peace treaty with Israel and world "security." The world is restless.

This is nothing new to the Lord.

Over 2,700 years ago He spoke through Isaiah to Israel who had placed their *confidence* in a treaty with Egypt instead of *confiding in Him.* The root word of "confidence" is "confide." To *be* confid-ent in Him is to confide your whole self, entrust your whole life to Him.

Mercifully, the Lord is still waiting for Israel, you, and me. He longs for you to truly *turn* to Him so He can bring you real rest, help, and the fruit of faithfulness.

So the LORD must wait for you to come to him so he can show you his love and compassion. For the LORD is a faithful God. Blessed are those who wait for his help. Isaiah 30:18

The Lord is a *faithful* God, a perfect leader for imperfect people. Will we place our confidence in His leadership?

Many years ago, I was pastor of a church that met in a large three-story building. One night we gathered our youth group in the sanctuary for a "trust walk." One person was to wear a blind fold and place their hand on the other's shoulder who would act as their guide. They were then led through hallways, up and down stairways, across unlevel floors, into far corners and odd nooks. If you have never done this try it sometime, it's quite a trip! Actually, the point is for the guide to carefully help the blindfolded person *not* trip! The process works best for the adult leaders to lead the blindfolded youth through the course once and then pair off the youth to do it for each other. It's interesting to watch how especially careful and attentive to detail each guide was *after* they had been led through the blindfold walk. They were acquainted with the fear, appreciative of trustworthy help.

It's a mystery, but true, that Jesus was fully man and fully God. We don't give Him enough credit for His faithfulness, His confident trust in His Father. We often act as if He was simply God walking around in a costume and life was easy for Him. The fact is the Bible says He was tempted in every way known to man. Yet He continually chose to trust His Father and only speak as He heard His Father speaking and only do what He saw His Father doing. He did not let his human needs, pains, emotions, or the devil lead Him around in His words or actions. In other words, Jesus was the first fully confid-ent "trustwalker"! The Bible says Jesus is the firstborn of many brothers and sisters. He longs for you to let Him *help* you follow Him. He has been through life, death, and resurrection from the dead. He knows how to help you get through all the ins and outs, all the ups and downs of this life all the way home. He is *completely* trustworthy and carefully attentive to all the details of your life. He knows what He is doing, especially when you don't know what to do.

It was one thing for me to explain to junior high kids how to do a trust walk through a big old building, but it was another thing for me to put on the blindfold myself and let one of the youth lead me around. I got in touch with my trust issues real quick!

What's keeping you from fully trusting the Lord? What are your present fears, your trust issues with the Lord?

He offers His love and compassion to personally guide you through life. The real fruit of faithfulness is confident trust in Him. The world would have you settle for the plastic fruit of determined self-confidence. The siren song is to believe in yourself, be a person of your word, never give up, buckle down, suck it up. These things are the world's best, but not His.

Instead, He wants to help you live continually confident in Him. He waits for you with open arms of love and compassion. He waits for you to utter one deep sincere word, "Help!" So often we will not.

The state of Israel still places its confidence in its military, allies like the U.S., and treaties as with Egypt. Most Americans affirm the Judeo-Christian roots of the United States yet we still place our real confidence in our military, technological, and economic "might." Increasingly secular thinking in America prizes such things as earthly democracy, freedom, environmentalism, or one world order rather than the Lord. Again, this is the world's best, not His. I am very grateful to be an American because no nation in history has been more blessed by the Lord and no nation in history has a better record of protecting one's freedom to worship the one true God known only through Jesus Christ. That being said, we are a nation that is sleep walking not trust walking. We need an awakening.

How can we help our nation become more faithful? Legislation, elections, or even revolution won't do it. Only the Lord can do it through individual hearts growing and linking in real fruit, real love—person by person, generation after generation. The Kingdom of God can come quickly, but it still comes one person at a time. Ask Him to grow you faithful.

To be faith-ful means to confidently trust the Lord by letting Him help you in every area of your life. Let the Lord grow you fruitful as a child of faith. He yearns for this. If you do not ask Him and let Him help you will experience needless adversity and suffering.

Yet, He waits. Look what He promises when you finally turn to Him and ask for help.

O people of Zion, who live in Jerusalem, you will weep no more. He will be gracious if you ask for help. He will surely respond to the sound of your cries. Though the Lord gave you adversity for food and suffering for drink, he will still be with you to teach you. You will see your teacher with your own eyes. Your own ears will hear him. Right behind you a voice will say, "This is the way you should go, whether to the right or to the left." Isaiah 30:19-21

Right now, if you ask Jesus to help you He *will* respond to your cries. Your asking opens your eyes and ears to see and hear Him with you. He is right there with you waiting. He will help you see and hear the way He wants you to go. He means exactly what He says. He is faithful to His word. He is faithful to His promises to you. Trust walk.

Remember, real fruit is the Holy Spirit coming forth in your words, deeds, and relationships. Therefore, the fruit of faithfulness means Jesus inspiring confidence in you and in others *through* you. His faithfulness is Him keeping His promises. Your faithfulness is not you keeping your promises, but you trusting Him to keep His promises in all your words and actions.

Plastic fruit is your determined self-confidence. There is not one place in Scripture where the Lord tells us to believe in ourselves. He does not expect us to pull ourselves up by our own bootstraps. Many people will say the Lord helps those who help themselves, but the Bible never says that! Isaiah is basically telling us the Lord helps those who *ask* Him for help! Believing in your self is the blindfolded leading the blindfolded. So is humanity trying to solve humanity's problems.

As a young pastor I knew a young high school teacher and coach who adamantly taught his athletes to believe in themselves. He had a well-intentioned desire to help his athletes overcome their fears in order to achieve success. This was not a bad thing according to worldly values; it just wasn't God's values. The world's best is still plastic fruit. Unbeknownst to most, the poor man was fighting his own tormented inner battles and really never let the Lord help him. Then one day he closed himself off from everyone and killed himself. Among the varied reasons and circumstances of suicide there is one common lie every suicidal person comes to believe with all their heart—"I'm all alone, no one cares, there is no hope." It was a shock to the whole community. At the funeral for this man who believed that lie, the Lord helped me speak these words:

None of us, particularly his family, would be going through this hell right now if our friend had not chosen to kill himself. He has left us sad, angry, and confused. Let's admit that to ourselves and to God. That's the first step to being able to forgive our friend. You athletes here know the value of his coaching and encouragement. What's confusing is what do you do with the fact that a man who lived and taught 'believe in yourself' then chooses to kill himself? The truth is there is only One person in the world who will never let you down; only One person who truly understands you; only One person who can help you truly become the person He made you to be. He's the only One person in whom you truly can believe. Jesus is the only person who can help you heal and live healthily through this tragedy, and any dark time of life. He's the only person who understands our friend's struggle. So into His hands let us commit our friend. Into His hands let us commit ourselves. Nothing can separate us from His love.

You may not be suicidal, but you probably know what it feels like to believe nobody cares, and that you are all alone in a circumstance. You may even know what it feels like to have no hope. Most definitely, in this famine of love there are several people in your neighborhood, school, or workplace who feel this way.

So stop for a moment, take a deep breath, exhale, and come rest in His love *and* perspective. Think about this. Whatever is going on in life, you can find yourself somewhere along the "continuum" between verses 15 and 23 in Isaiah 30. I have lived fifty-four years and am just now discovering how helpful this passage is in my trust walk toward real faithfulness.

For example, in verse 15, the Lord lays it out clearly. Everyone you know will be rudderless and restless until they truly return to the Lord. Those who *return* receive *rest.* We must return from all the "security" alliances we make with people, philosophies, or institutions. Is there any way in which you have made an alliance with someone or some group for your security? You will be constantly restless, subject to all kinds of fear if you confide the trust of your well being to anyone but Jesus.

Kim and I have discovered that we are free to love and enjoy one another in marriage if we place our security needs in Him rather than each other. So many marriages needlessly suffer and fail because couples expect their mate to be their "everything" rather than helping each other keep their eyes on the Lord as their all in all. For many of us, financial security is the alliance from which we must turn. A worldwide financial crash may, or may not be on the horizon, but it's "dog eat dog" already whenever we secretly place our faith in finances for security. Famine of love comes from such "alliances" with money, political parties, relationships, success, career, etc.

Some people place their well being in the well being of their children. Children are not to be worshiped, but loved. Some make the well-intentioned mistake of making an alliance of security with their church. No church, no organization, can be a substitute for the Living Christ. We are only at rest, free to love, when we have returned from all alliances.

What about you, the people in your sphere of influence? Ask the Lord to help you and everyonc around you leave their alliances and return to Him. Ask the Lord to set up conversations and opportunities to help people around you leave their alliances and return to the Lord. Watch what happens. It doesn't mean that you or they have to necessarily leave their organizations and associations to become hermits. Not at all! It means an exchange of heart. Who's got your heart really? Is it the Lord or someone or something else? Your answer lies within you as you consider how you spend your money, time, talents, your very life. He does not want you to give Him lip service; He wants the whole "enchilada"!

So the Isaiah 30 "continuum" looks like this:

Alliance---Return---Rest---Ask---Follow---Renounce---Plant---Harvest

At any given time, any one of us can progress or regress along this continuum. But there is always our amazing Lord offering amazing grace to help us along the way. What a Lord! That's why faithfulness is a personal and corporate reality in the Body of Christ. We need each other to help each other keep our eyes on Christ.

In the next chapter we will look at a couple ways to do this. For now, where are you on the continuum?

RETURN

Do you need to return to the Lord from an alliance? Ask Him to help you. Ask another believer to help you.

REST

Do you need to let go of control and rest in His love?

Resting isn't sleeping or passive. Surrender your burdens, surrender control, and surrender your focus to Him. Begin learning to let Him love you and lead you.

ASK

Do you need to ask Him for help? Do you go days, or even weeks, trying your best to be faithful without ever asking Him to actually *help* you do the things you are trying to do for Him! The Bible says we have not because we ask not.

FOLLOW

Do you long to see, hear, and truly follow the Lord in your life? Returning, resting, asking is His way of preparing you for Him to more deeply and clearly reveal Himself to you. There are as many ways He does this as there are people. The problem is most people don't trust Him this far along the continuum. I guarantee you, more important, HE guarantees you that He *will* show up!

RENOUNCE

Do you long to be rid of false idols, bad habits, addictions, or destructive attachments to things? Good news. Isaiah 30 dispels the religious lie that you have to set yourself free and clean yourself up, before the Holy Spirit will move in your life. The fact is that as you return, rest, ask, and follow, the Lord will meet you where you are and personally help you *completely destroy* evil in your life. You were made for embracing God and people, not for attaching to things. He will help you directly, and through His people to kick bad stuff out and *unlearn* fearful, coping, addictive behaviors that have built up over the years. Remember, your only identity is that of His beloved child. Many addicts trade one slavemaster for another. It's a good thing that a person stops drinking if they are addicted to alcohol. However, it is only the world's best to declare "I am a recovering alcoholic."

He wants to give you His best so you will declare "I am a beloved child of God, set free of addiction by Jesus Christ."

PLANT

Finally, the Lord wants to help you reap the reward of His investment of love in you. He wants to help you plant seeds of real love that only you can plant through your life with Him. He wants you to use the desires, abilities, and power He has given you to pour yourself freely into the lives of others.

HARVEST

As you give with no strings attached He pours out His presence on your work and great fruitfulness will abound.

This is the Lord's path to a faithful life. The more you trust Him the more He can lead you to bless others along the "continuum."

Then you will destroy all your silver idols and your precious gold images. You will throw them out like filthy rags, saying to them, "Good riddance!" Then the LORD will bless you with rain at planting time. There will be wonderful harvests and plenty of pastureland for your livestock. Isaiah 30:22-23

So wherever you are that's where He is. Trust. Walk. Grow full of faith.

Chapter 24
Go Deeper

Blessed is the man who trusts in the LORD, And whose hope is the LORD. For he shall be like a tree planted by the waters, Which spreads out its roots by the river, And will not fear when heat comes; But its leaf will be green, And will not be anxious in the year of drought, Nor will cease from yielding fruit.

—Jeremiah 17:7-8 NKJV

The movie *Bottleshock* tells the humorous story of obscure, struggling vintners in California whose wine won a shocking victory in a blind taste test against world famous vintners in France in the 1970s. Napa Valley is now world renowned. At one point, the Napa vintner takes on an intern even though the business is struggling. He is passionate about grape growing and wants to impart that passion. As he walks with the intern through the vineyard on her first day he says something which is the core message of the film. He tells her the right kind of soil for growing grapes must be loose and dry so the vine roots have to struggle down deep for their water source. If the topsoil is wet they don't have to struggle and the grapes do not reach their potential.

Without struggle, growing down deep in faithfulness to Jesus Christ, no one can become what they were created by Him to be. Are you struggling to grow in faithfulness to Jesus? Be encouraged. The Lord struggled on the cross for you. He wants you to know your struggle to keep following Him is worth it.

Therefore, having been justified by faith, we have peace with God through our Lord Jesus Christ, through whom also we have access by faith into this grace in which we stand, and rejoice in hope of the glory of God. And not only that, but we also glory in tribulations, knowing that tribulation produces perseverance; and perseverance, character; and character, hope. Now hope does not disappoint, because the love of God has been poured out in our hearts by the Holy Spirit who was given to us. Romans 5:1-5 NKJV

Jesus struggled and died for you and sent the Holy Spirit to invite you to entrust your life to Him. In your first moment of faith, the Holy Spirit came into your heart and filled you with Jesus' love. You were made right in the Father's sight by Jesus' blood sacrifice. Since then the Lord has been working 24/7 to help your roots grow deep to become a deeply loving child. The fruit of faithfulness is growing ever deeper roots in Jesus.

Jeremiah lived in a time when Israel had stopped struggling to put down its roots in God's love. They had strayed from God and were about to be destroyed. It is painfully true that God's people can harden their hearts and reject Him and receive disaster. Yet, the Lord continued to be faithful in the face of Israel's faithlessness and spoke dire warning through Jeremiah. He also lovingly offered a promise of hope for anyone who would listen to Jeremiah—then and now.

The Lord knows your weakness, but does expect you to fight to become more like Him. Resting in Jesus is not passive, but passionate trust in Him. When you truly sign on with Him all the forces of hell are against you because when you bear the fruit of the Spirit, people get saved. You can trust Him to defend you.

The Lord tells us in 1 Corinthians 13 that everything in life comes down to faith, hope, and love. God's love is where we came from and Heaven is our hope if we truly have a faith relationship with Jesus. Simply put, "faith" is trusting Jesus' unfailing love moment by moment and "hope" is trusting He will be there for you at the end.

Jeremiah says if you trust and hope in the Lord you will become as a deep rooted tree that never dries up, never blows down, and always bears fruit no matter the drought. The soil for those deep roots is Limitless Love.

Look at this prayer of Paul for the Ephesians. Memorize it one verse a week until it's in your heart. Pray this once a day for yourself and often for as many people as you can the rest of your life. This is what Jesus came to do for all who trust Him.

I pray that from his glorious, unlimited resources he will empower you with inner strength through his Spirit. Then Christ will make his home in your hearts as you trust in him. Your roots will grow down into God's love and keep you strong. And may you have the power to understand, as all God's people should, how wide, how long, how high, and how deep his love is. May you experience the love of Christ, though it is too great to understand fully. Then you will be made complete with all the fullness of life and power that comes from God. Ephesians 3:16-19

Faith, hope, and love. Trust His love now, trust His love at the end, become His love for others. That's his way. He is not a fairweather friend and wants you to be a fruitful friend no matter sun or storm. The Lord is always faithful to you not because bad things never happen, but because He says so in the Bible. To trust Him is to trust His word.

And we know that God causes everything to work together for the good of those who love God and are called according to his purpose for them. For God knew his people in advance, and he chose them to become like his Son, so that his Son would be the firstborn among many brothers and sisters. Romans 8:28-29

Trust Him to be faithful in all circumstances to make you Christlike. Such trust is the only thing that pleases Him.

And without faith it is impossible to please him, for whoever would draw near to God must believe that he exists and that he rewards those who seek him. Hebrews 11:6 ESV

He's not looking for your perfect performance. He simply wants to be trusted. The way you show Jesus you love Him is to trust Him. The way you show your trust is to follow His commandments. The Holy Spirit will help you every step.

If you love me, you will keep my commandments. And I will ask the Father, and he will give you another Helper, to be with you forever. John 14:15-16 ESV

He will continue to teach you trust by testing you in your triumphs and failures. Being a lifelong disciple of Jesus simply means receiving His love and giving His love no matter what happens. Being His disciple is not a sprint through flowery meadows, but a marathon over high mountains and through deep valleys and everything in between.

The devil will tempt you to believe that bad things mean the Lord is not faithful. Here is the truth:

If we endure hardship, we will reign with him. If we deny him, he will deny us. If we are unfaithful, he remains faithful, for he cannot deny who he is. Remind everyone about these things, and command them in God's presence to stop fighting over words. Such arguments are useless, and they can ruin those who hear them. 2 Timothy 2:12-14

Famine of love deepens when our faith roots don't! Claiming to have faith and real faithfulness are different things. Faithfulness is not static. The fruit is either growing or dying. At any given time you are either growing in faithfulness or losing faith. Faithfulness is obedience, the Holy Spirit helps you do what Jesus commands.

Going to church is plastic fruit if you aren't really going to Jesus. Sometimes churches don't preach the real gospel and don't help people receive and give real love. It's possible to go to church and go to hell. It's possible to begin with Jesus, become bitter, hardened, and walk away from Him. All the while friends and family remain in famine of love. Life is a war for souls.

For it is impossible to bring back to repentance those who were once enlightened—those who have experienced the good things of heaven and shared in the Holy Spirit, who have tasted the goodness of the word of God and the power of the age to come—and who then turn away from God. It is impossible to bring such people back to repentance; by rejecting the Son of God, they themselves are nailing him to the cross once again and holding him up to public shame. Hebrews 6:4-6

Jesus wants no life ruined. Someone who once believed but has now rejected Him can be like a wolf in sheep's clothing and lead many astray. Jesus reserves His harshest promises for the devil and anyone else who becomes a true threat to His little ones.

Do not be frightened, yet have a healthy fear and trust in Him. The fact that you are reading this book is proof Jesus loves you and is helping you put down deeper roots. You need never fear falling away as long as the thought of it is too horrible to contemplate. Remember the Holy Spirit lives in believers. He is not going to sit idle if we start turning away. He will convict us within and prompt other believers to care for us. He will fight for us, but never force us to believe.

Will you choose to trust He is faithful even when bad things happen? Do you trust Him to see you through and be there for you when you die?

Once, after three years of intense circumstances in which the Lord was testing me to put down deeper roots, I found myself in the third chapter of Lamentations of Jeremiah. Yes, the same Jeremiah who knew the importance of faith, hope, and deep roots in God's love. This is from the prayer cry of Jeremiah when everything fell apart around him and his nation:

I am the man who has seen affliction under the rod of his wrath; he has driven and brought me into darkness without any light; surely against me he turns his hand again and again the whole day long. He has made my flesh and my skin waste away; he has broken my bones; he has besieged and enveloped me with bitterness and tribulation; he has made me dwell in darkness like the dead of long ago. He has walled me about so that I cannot escape; he has made my chains heavy; though I call and cry for help, he shuts out my prayer; he has blocked my ways with blocks of stones; he has made my paths crooked .He has made my teeth grind on gravel, and made me cower in ashes;

my soul is bereft of peace; I have forgotten what happiness is; so I say, "My endurance has perished; so has my hope from the LORD." Lamentations 3:1-18 ESV

What a passage. When pressed upon on all sides, Jeremiah did not doubt or reject the Lord, he cried out in lament. The next time the Lord allows painful circumstances in your life, if necessary do the faithful thing—lament. Lament is not complaining about the Lord. Lament is crying out in pain *to* the Lord. Lament is fruitful. When you lament, your roots of faith go down deeper in Him.

When I read this lament of Jeremiah I fell on my face and repented from my self-pity and realized three powerful truths. Though He has tested me, He has never yet put me through what He put Jeremiah and Israel through. I am very grateful for His mercy. Second, He actually went through all this and even more for me on the Cross! Third, I could now see from His perspective on those three years that His hand was in all of it. In a very deep and loving way, He led me into testing circumstances *so* I would struggle and grow in the fruit of faithfulness.

For the sake of others in the days ahead, I will need deeper roots. So will you.

If you trust that challenging circumstances are a test from Him that He wants you to walk through *with* Him—then you will never doubt or reject the Lord. Never forget the devil only tempts you if the Lord allows it. Wherever the lying tempter moves, the Faithful Tester is right there to help you choose faith, hope, and love! Going through trials perfectly in your own strength is *not* passing the test. Leaning on Jesus all the way *is!* Bank on it!

Then as I read through the rest of the third chapter of Lamentations I was blown away.

This I recall to my mind, Therefore I have hope. Through the LORD's mercies we are not consumed, Because His compassions fail not. They are new every morning; Great is Your faithfulness. Lamentations 3:21-23 NKJV

Only after Jeremiah entered the valley of lament did the Lord then take him to a fresh revelation of His loving faithfulness! The Lord will never let you down. He may take you down into a dark valley but only for the purpose of faith, hope, and love. The greatest of these is love. Never fear the going deeper. It's all worth it for you and those around you.

Great is His faithfulness. Trusting Him, great will be yours.

It is good to give thanks to the LORD And to sing praises to Your name, O Most High; To declare Your loving kindness in the morning And Your faithfulness by night. Psalm 92:1-3 NASB

Chapter 25

20/20/20

If you abide in me, and my words abide in you, ask whatever you wish, and it will be done for you.

—John 15:7 NKJV

20/20/20 is a plan for daily hang time with your Best Friend. The more time you spend with the Lord the deeper your roots go down in Him, the more His joy strengthens you. I call it 20/20/20 because He sharpens your spiritual vision when you do it and it's quantity and quality time to hang with Him, chew His words, and pray with Him for real fruit. Do you spend one hour alone with the Lord each day? If not, here is a practical way to do so. If so, great! Consider adding another hour!

Do you think I'm crazy? He's crazier. He actually believes that He can bring you into a future when you are full of His joy no matter what circumstances arise. The more you hang out with Him the more your life will bring lush hanging fruit on the vine for others. What have you got to lose except a bunch of stumbling, bumbling, joyless, shallow roots living?

Follow these steps.

1. Set a daily appointment with the Lord you never break without His permission, preferably the first full hour of your day. If you don't think you have the time, get up one hour earlier and go to bed one hour earlier. Is He worth the adjustment?
2. Do this in a quiet room where you will not be interrupted. Your friends and family will respect and appreciate this as they benefit from your increased joy.
3. Bring your Bible, a notebook, pen, a timer or automatic alarm, and your hungry heart for more of Him.
4. Sit upright in a chair with good back support. Don't lie down or you will go to sleep. Place your hands in your lap or on the arms of the chair, whatever is comfortable.
5. Set your timer or alarm for twenty minutes. If you are using your phone, put everything but the alarm on "silent." My wife Kim enjoys playing heartfelt praise or instrumental music beforehand as preparation. I prefer beginning in silence. Experiment to find which works for you. See yourself sitting face to face with Jesus. Thank the Lord for watching over you in the night and for the wonderful day He has prepared for you.
6. Start the timer, close your eyes, and begin twenty minutes of silent prayer centering yourself in Jesus' arms of love.

- Begin by praying aloud, "Holy Spirit come touch my life."
- Be still and simply trust the Holy Spirit is moving in you as He wants.

- You may or may not be comfortable with silence. That's okay, He is comfortable and will help you. Keep your eyes closed during the entire twenty minutes to avoid visual distractions.
- If thoughts or images rise up within your mind simply see yourself letting them go into Jesus' hands. Many people let rising thoughts distract and defeat their attempts to rest in the Lord in silence. You don't ever have to fear distractions again. You have asked the Holy Spirit to move in you and you can trust that any thought coming to mind is a thought He simply wants you to surrender to Jesus. Give it to Him. But if you find it difficult and you start "dwelling" upon that thought—then simply call aloud, "Jesus!" He will help you get back to "dwelling" on Him. You may need to call out His name many times or none at all. You have nothing to prove to anyone except showing Him you love Him and want to rest with Him. One of the sure signs of a real friendship is that you simply enjoy hanging out.
- When the timer rings, pray aloud the Lord's Prayer. But remember this is His prayer. In Matthew 6 He tells us to not pray in vain repetitions. So don't do that with His words. Say one phrase at a time and pause in silence a moment before you go on to the next phrase. Enjoy the Holy Spirit. Enjoy praying with Jesus.
- The more you do this, the more peaceful and patient you will become.

7. Open your Bible and notebook. Set the timer for another twenty minutes. Asking the Lord to speak to your heart.

- Open up to any book of the Bible. Try Psalms, John, or Philippians for starters. All Scripture is alive and packed with Jesus' love. Read slowly with an open heart. Try not to read more than six verses in the time allotted. It's not how much Scripture you cruise through, but how much Scripture sinks into you. Remember, He wants His words to abide, live in you.
- Read one verse slowly in silence. Repeat it aloud. Wait. Chew on it. See if the Lord draws your attention to a particular, word, phrase, or concept. The Bible word "meditate" means to chew like a cow chews the cud. Sounds a little gross, but the Lord's word is plenty earthy! For His word to abide in you means you need to chew slowly, swallow, and bring it up again to get all the nutrients. This gives the Holy Spirit a chance to bring instructive thoughts and pictures to your mind that apply to your life. The more you do this the more you will begin to feel the Lord's pleasure. His word says it is impossible to please Him except by faith. The way you show Him you love Him is to show Him you trust Him by doing what He says. Your chewing is doing what He says. Joy will rise. It's great!
- As you read write down any words, phrases, or pictures that are coming to your mind in the fruit of the Spirit—words that seem loving, joyful, peaceful, patient, kind, faithful, good, humble, or pure. To be able to track a growing conversation with Him, write the thoughts that seem to be coming from Him in printing. Write the thoughts that seem to be yours in cursive. This simple technique of journaling can help you get in the habit of conversing with Him all day. If you love Jesus, then there are two voices inside you. His voice

always tells you to do what the Bible says. Your voice tends to tell you what you want to do. The Holy Spirit always speaks with one or more of His nine fruit. Since He breathed all Scripture, He never says anything contrary to His word. Abiding in Him means you are learning to constantly yield your will to His. The more you chew and digest Scripture the more He will help you grow confident in, and sensitive to, His voice. You will be on your way to a true Spirit-led life of real joy! Yes, Satan can throw temptations and lies at us. Whenever that happens just take them to Jesus. He will help you resist the devil who will then flee. The more you do this, the more you will defeat the enemy throughout the day.

- As you chew, digest, and journal through the verses, open your heart to Him and ask Him to heal any wounds He seems to be shining light on. Think of yourself like his little child with a scraped knee. You need to expose the wound to your Jesus so He can cleanse it and kiss it and make it all better.
- Ask Him if there is anything else He wants to say.
- Rest with Him and ponder the verses and thoughts in silence. He will be moving deeply in ways you may, or may not, be aware.
- When the timer goes off, take a moment and review any action steps for the day He may have revealed. Do them today. Also, review the verses you chewed. Does one stand out? Break it down into three parts. Begin memorizing it by repeating it aloud. Write it down on a separate paper. Ask the Lord to help you memorize it today. The Bible calls this "hiding it in your heart." Once you memorize a verse, the Holy Spirit can bring it back to your mind whenever you need it.

8. Set your timer for the last twenty minutes. Ask the Holy Spirit to lead you in prayer for others and yourself.

- This is different than your prayer list. This is letting Him bring His prayer list to you! Be prepared to pray aloud. He will train you to be a confident prayer warrior in private and public.
- Sit and wait for Him to bring someone's face to your mind. Say, "Lord, please give me Your heart for this person. He may bring certain Scriptures to mind. Look it up. Pray for each person according to the fruit of the Spirit for His will for the good things from that passage. He may remind you of something you already knew to pray for. He may show you something you didn't know. If that happens, simply pray, "Lord, I place this matter and this person in your loving hands." If you are comfortable, feel free to simply pray in tongues for them. Ask Him if there is anything else. Wait. If nothing else comes, ask Him to give them life and life more abundant in Jesus' name. Write down any Scriptures or words of encouragement for them that are in line with the nine fruit of the Spirit.
- Ask, who's next Lord? Repeat the above.
- Ask, what's next Lord? He may bring local, national, or world situations to mind. Ask Him to bring Scriptures to mind. Pray in the real fruit of the Spirit according to those Scriptures.
- Repeat the process until the timer goes off.
- Pray the Lord's Prayer slowly again.

9. Ask the Lord to lead you throughout the day.

The more you practice with Him the more you will look forward to your time with Him. You will be amazed at how fast the hour goes and He will show you how to spend even more time with Him. Watch the way He changes you and blesses others through you. Each new day will be more power packed with real fruit.

Apart from Him you can do nothing. Abiding in Him you can do everything that matters.

He was hanged on a tree for you for three hours. Will you hang at least one with Him?

GENTLENESS

Real Gentleness: Other-serving Humility

Plastic Gentleness: Self-serving Politeness

Chapter 26
Going Low

Peter said to him, "Lord, are you going to wash my feet?" Jesus replied, "You don't understand now what I am doing, but someday you will."

—John 13:6-7

Shortly after my first book was published, I was invited to our church bookstore for a book signing. A woman in her late twenties came up to me with her husband. She asked, "Do you have any counsel for me on how to overcome writer's block? It is my deepest desire to write for the Lord but I just can't seem to get unstuck. Has that ever happened to you and do you have any advice?"

As I listened to her I immediately saw a picture in my mind of the young woman seated in a chair with Jesus kneeling before her offering to wash her feet. So I suggested she experiment with something.

I asked her to go home to where she normally would write at her computer, laptop, or desk. Instead of writing though, I encouraged her to relax, close her eyes, and have prayer conversation with Jesus, seeing and trusting that He was at her feet looking up into her eyes with His eyes of love. I asked her to *ask Him* what was blocking her writing. I asked her to let Him care for her and talk with her.

She cut me off waving her hands and saying, "Oh no, I could never see Jesus at my feet. He is the exalted One!!" There was the beginning of tears in her eyes. I said, "Oh but dear one that is precisely why He is the Exalted One, because He humbled Himself on the Cross for us. He is the Risen One who still goes low for you and me and everyone! He always goes lower than we do. He loves you so. He will show you." I prayed for her and her husband and we all shared hugs with tears and love. It was quite a moment of "washing" and new understanding.

There really is only one person who will ever truly "understand" you—the One who is standing under you. He is the One who made you with love, who died to save you with love, who longs to lead you with love forever. Let Him.

Several years ago, I began to see Jesus' assumed position in our lives is at our feet. I am learning to see Him that way in my prayer life and I encourage you to try it. Not as the only way you see Jesus in your life, but one deep lifesaving way… especially when you need to be "understood."

So often I lived my life for days, weeks, and years on end trying my best to serve Jesus when that is really His job, not mine. He says in John 16, I no longer call you servants, I call you my friends. He said He came to serve, not be served. We often make the jump to thinking we need to strive to serve others like Jesus did, but we forget to let Him fulfill His mission with us.

For even the Son of Man came not to be served but to serve others and to give his life as a ransom for many." Matthew 20:28

One of the many awesome things about Jesus is He turns our religious striving and perceptions upside down. You get to permanently rest from striving to serve God in your own power. Your calling is to be served by Jesus, to be His beloved. He told Peter he could have no part in Him unless He washed him.

So many people are afraid to surrender to Jesus as their Lord because they don't realize the kind of Lord he is. That's because too few of us believers let Jesus serve us. In Isaiah, the Bible says one day there would come a Suffering Servant who would save us by taking all our sin and disease upon Himself. Guess who?

So many non-Christians never get to see Christians totally ablaze with the love of Christ because most Christians won't spend their days letting Jesus love them. Most of us don't give Him a chance because we have settled for a cheap substitute, an almost "plastic Jesus." Take Him at his word. His continuing mission, through the Holy Spirit is to serve *you.* If you let Him, He will release the fruit and gifts of His Spirit in all your living.

The reason He has been given Lordship *over* all things is because He submitted, went as low as necessary to redeem all things. If you surrender to the real Jesus, He will not Lord over you, he will Lord *under* you! And you can rest secure in His everlasting arms of love under you.

So many Christians run around with deep shame and despair for always falling short, always letting the Lord down. I once heard Pastor Rick Warren say, "You can't let God down, because you aren't holding him up!" So wise.

It is true that we all fall short of God's glory. But, in Jesus, God's love never falls short of us!

You might say, "But aren't we supposed to serve God? Didn't Paul describe himself as a 'bondservant.'" That is true only because Paul was so overwhelmed by how much the Lord loved him in every way he did not deserve. Paul knew he had been bought at a great price—the Suffering Servant had died for His sins and lovingly confronted him on the road to Damascus.

Paul, before he surrendered to the Lord, was actually persecuting the Risen Jesus by terrorizing the early Christians in whom Jesus lived. You are free to describe yourself as the Lord's servant as long as you remember Jesus describes you as His friend as an expression of your true relationship with Him. Again, the paradox, I really want to serve an exalted God Who wants nothing more than to humbly serve me as His friend! How about you?

Several years ago, our friend heard her young daughter singing with great gusto a praise song in the next room, "He is exhausted the King is exhausted on high, I will praise Him. He is exhausted, forever exhausted and I will praise His name!"

This was so hilarious because the child was so wholeheartedly singing a word she misunderstood from Twila Paris' wonderful song "He Is Exalted!" Hilarious, yes! Yet the child really had it right in such a deep way. Jesus the King was exalted by His Father, because He allowed Himself to be completely exhausted, completely poured out unto death on the cross for us.

The Suffering Servant understands your exhaustion with trying to be a good person, with trying to cope with this love starved world, with trying to grow yourself. Come to Him, He will give you a life of rest from striving and you will begin thriving in all the ways that really matter. The King was exhausted once for all, but He will never die nor be exhausted again. Will you change the way you think and begin letting Him serve you? Out of the overflow of receiving you will find yourself carried, as upon a wave, into the joy of serving others in an inexhaustible love that never falls short even when you do.

So before you go to the next chapter of this book, before you begin each day, take a few moments, close your eyes, let go and trust that the Lord is kneeling in front of you. Let down your guard and ask Him if He has anything to show you. Tell Him what's on your mind. Let go.

Let's pray:

Lord, I'll cut to the chase. I really want to be your friend. But I know I don't deserve You. I'm afraid I will not hold up my end of the bargain. Help me stop bargaining. I am afraid of ending up as a selfish empty person. I surrender. Please heal my aching heart. I'm tired of trying to make myself a better person. I give you permission to serve me. Help me with this. Like Peter, I have some un-learning to do. I take you at your word. I want to let You be Yourself and do Your thing. Have at it. Wash me with your amazing love. Amen.

CHAPTER 27

EVEN WHEN WE DISAGREE

What is causing the quarrels and fights among you?...You are jealous of what others have... so you fight... to take it away from them. Yet you don't have what you want because you don't ask God for it. And even when you ask, you don't get it because your motives are all wrong—you want only what will give you pleasure... Don't you realize that friendship with the world makes you an enemy of God?...But he gives us even more grace to stand against such evil desires. As the Scriptures say, "God opposes the proud but favors the humble." So humble yourselves before God. Resist the devil, and he will flee from you. Come close to God, and God will come close to you. Wash your hands, you sinners; purify your hearts, for your loyalty is divided between God and the world.

—James 4:1-8

Many years ago I was pastor of a large church with beautiful stained glass in an old majestic sanctuary with a high pulpit backed by a two-sided antiphonal choir loft. One Sunday morning in worship I had just finished teaching and praying with a large group of small children on the floor down by the front pews and was ascending back up the steps to the pulpit.

Suddenly I heard the quarreling and shouting of two *very* familiar voices. I wheeled around to see only two children had not yet returned to their seats—my own precious five-year-old daughter and my precious three -year-old son—squabbling like cats and dogs for all the world to see! Kids being kids, except all eyes are on the preacher's kids being kids! My wife saw them first but she was still seated in the choir loft as the choir had not yet sung their anthem. When she tried to exit the choir loft her ornery friend stuck her leg out blocking the way. All this played out in the instant I realized my young sister-in-law, with whom our kids were sitting, was not yet responding. In those days I wore a traditional black pulpit robe and the style of that service was dignified and a little stiff. No doubt there were many in the crowd quietly chuckling and many others waiting to see what would happen. But it was clear to me in this instant that plain ol' Dad, not the high pulpit preacher, needed to swoop down and deal with his children just as he would in his own back yard. I got to them just as the quarrel was escalating. I put my face between them and took their hands and spoke very firmly and quietly in "Dad tone" to "stop this right now!" They stopped instantly and I marched them back to my sister-in-law. And that was that. Quarrel over, smiles and tittering continuing all around.

The Lord helped me learn a lesson and pass a test that day. Real love proceeds regardless what people think. Real love quiets quarreling people and walks them away from their worst selves toward their better selves.

A gentle answer deflects anger, but harsh words make tempers flare. Proverbs 15:1

Gentleness is a fruit of the Spirit and the opposite of quarreling. If I lovingly disagree with you it means I am at rest in the Lord's arms and free to gently invite you to consider my viewpoint. My desire is to love you regardless of your response, rather than to get you to come over to my view. The Lord will ultimately prove to both of us what is right so we don't have to stress and strain in the meantime.

There is a famine of real gentleness in public discourse today. Politics and the news media thrive on fear fed quarreling. There is such a critical spirit thriving in the world because our rebellious wills are always casting about for something to kill our pain and give us pleasure. Misery loves company so we align ourselves in political and theological camps where we can feed off each other's insecurities. We belittle one another to bolster ourselves, instead of humbling ourselves to help one another.

Since the Lord convicted me to no longer watch television news or listen to talk radio, I am much less fearful and critical and much more peaceful and gentle on a daily basis. We don't need all the media input the world says we need. Some media can be helpful. But your time can be better spent enjoying the Lord, sweet company of family and friends, a good book, a beautiful sunset, a starry night, helping a hurting person, or precious silence. When you feed on fear and seething criticism in media, you can't bring the real fruit of Jesus to love starved people. Insecurity leads us to fill our lives with gunk. Jesus leads us to fill our lives with Him! Ask the Holy Spirit to show you how much media input He wants you to receive.

Rest from your fear of missing out on information. Rest from your fear of missing out on fun. That's really what's involved in rebellion. We think we know better than God. When you are quick to be critical of the Bible you will be quick to be critical of people.

Come rest from open mindedness to *everything*. The Bible says to open your mind only to those things that are of God.

Think about the things of heaven, not the things of earth. For you died to this life, and your real life is hidden with Christ in God. Colossians 3:2-3

I used to prize the plastic fruit of "open-mindedness" and criticize and label as "close-minded" everyone who did not agree with my political and theological camp. The Lord patiently showed me over the years the emotional insecurities and spiritual bankruptcy of such a stance. His words in the Bible are filled with real truth, mercy, and life to set all of us free from sin.

It's unloving to pursue a mindset that truth is relative and every person is their own god. We can become so judgmental that we accuse everyone who differs with us as being judgmental! This can lead us to regularly hate public officials and other precious souls simply because they are in the opposite political party. An insecure person is inclined to fear everything but the Lord.

Do not fear those who can kill the body. Fear only the One who can destroy both body and soul in hell forever... so fear not little flock! Matthew 10:28 NKJV

Jesus says the only one you need to fear is Him! But you don't have to be afraid because He has overcome sin, death, and fear on the Cross. Let Him love you and run your life and you never have to be afraid again. You never have to get caught up in the hateful, fearful insecurities of quarreling and rebellion. You can be free to flow full of His loving, joyful Spirit. You can end the famine of love and replace hateful rhetoric in public discourse with truly loving, respectful disagreement!

For Jesus is the one referred to in the Scriptures... There is salvation in no one else! God has given no other name under heaven by which we must be saved. Acts 4:11-12

The Lord wants you to seek His guidance and permission as to how you spend the precious twenty-four hours He gives you each day. But, quite honestly, we most often don't want to! There is a famine of love because we are too willfully distracted and woefully divided.

It's time we stop fighting like cats and dogs and start loving like Dad's grateful kids. The unbelieving world is watching and waiting for something better than its vain pursuits. When we Christians truly leave our insecurities behind—many secular people will leave their useless camps and join us in a heartbeat.

Can we agree to stop being disagreeable and start being teachable?

Chapter 28
The Real Deal

Beware of false prophets, who come to you in sheep's clothing, but inwardly they are ravenous wolves. You will know them by their fruits. Do men gather grapes from thornbushes or figs from thistles?

—Matthew 7:15-16 NKJV

My Grandma's house was one of my favorite places to be. I remember one hot summer day, walking down the steps into her cool basement to "help" with her canning. She spent a lot of time canning, because my Grandpa George spent a lot of time gardening. My grandparents had a huge garden full of a wide variety of fruits and vegetables all ripening at different times of summer.

The garden was always a big deal to me because I was a city kid raised by two loving parents who worked outside the home with no time to garden. Instead of store bought canned foods, Grandma had "real" green beans, "real" tomatoes, "real" corn on the cob. Kim still laughs when I call her mashed potatoes "real." I am of a vintage when it was all the rage for working parents to make instant mashed potatoes. I appreciate the real thing when it's put on my plate! So do most people, whether they are believers or not. Real spiritual fruit looks, feels, and tastes different from the quick stuff!

Taste and see that the LORD is good. Oh, the joys of those who take refuge in him! Psalm 34:8

Of all my favorite "real things" Grandma canned, the ultimate was her plum butter. One of the rewards of "helping" Grandma was being invited to pull up a chair and have her plum butter on bread. I've never tasted its equal. It was the combination of her particular tree and her particular recipe. There never has been and never will be that combination again. When you stop and think about it, there will only ever be one Jesus and one you! The combination of the two of you in a growing relationship can produce an awesome recipe of love for people around you! Truly the real thing! Real gentleness is real humility—the freedom to be your best self in Christ at all times.

When I think back, the garden and my grandma's house were a big deal to me because my grandparents were the *real* deal. Grandpa George was actually my step-grandfather but was a true grandpa to me since he married Grandma before I was born. He had smiling eyes and deep-voiced contagious laughter. Grandpa was the real deal who loved Jesus and knew He had spared his life on at least two occasions in World War II. Grandpa was in the U.S. Army 57th Signal Battalion and participated in five beach invasions of Nazi strongholds (North Africa, Sicily, Salerno, Anzio, and South France). Like many of his generation, he would simply say in his slow laughing drawl, "Aw, I was just a truck driver." Thanks Grandpa, you served your country and my Grandma well.

Grandma was Edith—a beautiful, fiery, fun loving woman of deep faith and sparkling eyes. During the Depression she was highly respected in her little town. She was a loving, prayerful wife and mama who worked her fingers to the bone taking in laundry and cleaning houses while her first husband, my Grandpa Frank, worked on the WPA and painted houses.

Grandma trooped on to feed her children bodily and spiritually. Every Sunday she gathered her six children to go to the little white frame Congregational church to learn of Jesus and His love. One day the pastor presented my mother with her first Bible. The inscription read "This book will keep you from sin. Sin will keep you from this book."

Grandma favorite hymn was "Take the Name of Jesus With You." As a young preacher, I always had my church sing it whenever she visited.

Take the name of Jesus with you, child of sorrow and of woe.
It will joy and comfort give you, take it then where'er you go.
Precious name, o how sweet, hope of earth and joy of heaven!
Precious name, o how sweet, hope of earth and joy of heaven!"

Grandma was the real deal because she knew the joy of what it meant to be a child of sorrow and woe who was loved, saved, and comforted by her Jesus! She became the spiritual leader of our large close extended family and I know the Lord used her faith, love, and prayers to draw me toward my destiny in Him. Grandma knew she was not perfect, but she would always be the first person in our family to declare Jesus was! She was not "holier than thou" but she knew she was holier than she used to be because of His love and guidance. In later years, she was never happier than when her five adult daughters would pull up a chair around her table with us all looking on as they led us in four part harmony singing gospel hymns like "There's Power in the Blood."

Would you be free from the burden of sin?
There's power in the blood, power in the blood;
Would you o'er evil a victory win?
There's wonderful power in the blood.

There is power, power, wonder working power
In the blood of the Lamb;
There is power, power, wonder working power
In the precious blood of the Lamb.

It's not lost on me that many years after Grandma's passing, I have now come to boldly believe more and more in the miraculous power of His precious blood. The Holy Spirit was planting seeds of real faith in me around that table of harmony.

It took the Holy Spirit several years to bring me as a pastor back to those good roots and to Him as my first love—trusting His loving miraculous presence. Many people in our churches came to hunger with me for more of the power of Jesus' wonderworking blood.

One day a few years ago, while walking in the woods I felt like the Lord spoke to my heart about the fruit of the Spirit in Galatians 5 and the gifts of the Spirit in 1 Corinthians 12. He brought the picture of a balance scale to mind and I saw that the nine fruit weighed heavier than the nine gifts. His people are more divided over His gifts but *more fearful* about His fruit. People can be afraid of the gifts they have not yet experienced and can be prideful about the gifts they have experienced. This causes division amongst His children and heartache to Him. However, He showed me His people are actually more afraid of the fruit of the Holy Spirit than the gifts. We all say we want more love, joy, peace, patience, kindness, goodness, faithfulness, gentleness, and self-control. However, to bear His fruit we have to change—we have to die to self to rise in His love. Often we won't.

If I speak in the tongues of men and of angels, but have not love, I am a noisy gong or a clanging cymbal. And if I have prophetic powers, and understand all mysteries and all knowledge, and if I have all faith, so as to remove mountains, but have not love, I am nothing. If I give away all I have, and if I deliver up my body to be burned, but have not love, I gain nothing. 1 Corinthians 13:1-4 ESV

Without love, real fruit, the gifts are nothing. If you speak in tongues from a loving heart it can be real. Making the same sounds from an angry heart is gibberish. Praying healing from an unmerciful, unbelieving, or impure heart is to no avail. Speaking a prophetic word, dream, or vision without kindness is not Him. His real love confirms the authenticity of His real gifts.

In this famine of love, many are wounded and afraid of those claiming to be "operating in the gifts." Yet in their fear they may shut themselves off from the Real Giver who operates through His children with His real gifts. It's okay. The Lord doesn't want us being carried away by false prophesy, false gifts, or even false fruit! Just don't shut yourself off in fear from the real taters, the real plum butter, the real thing!!

The Holy Spirit has not stopped releasing supernatural gifts. He wants His children to stop both denying and misusing the gifts and start bearing the Giver's real fruit. Where there is His real fruit growing there will be His real gifts flowing!

In the days to come, He will help us end the famine of love through His fruit often expressed through His gifts. There are other expressions of the fruit of the Spirit besides the gifts. However, if any of the nine gifts of the Spirit is real it will always be expressed lovingly, joyfully, peacefully, patiently, kindly, faithfully, generously, humbly, and with self-control. Bank on it! In this famine of love, let's believe in the reality of the gifts released through us by the Giver who always does it with love!

He is the real thing. Would you join me at His banquet table? There's always real taters, real plum butter, real fruit, real gifts. There's only one Perfect One at the table and lots of real love for all us imperfect children. His is the only real Tree of Life!

There is power in the precious blood of the Lamb. Precious Name, oh how *sweet.*

Don't miss your invitation. Pull up a chair.

The Angel said to me, "Write this: 'Blessed are those invited to the Wedding Supper of the Lamb.'" He added, "These are the true words of God!" Revelation 19:9, The Message

SELF-CONTROL

Real Self-Control:
Purity Promptings

Plastic Self-Control:
Self-discipline

Chapter 29

Doctor's Orders

But when the teachers of religious law who were Pharisees saw him eating with tax collectors and other sinners, they asked his disciples, "Why does he eat with such scum?" When Jesus heard this, he told them, "Healthy people don't need a doctor—sick people do. I have come to call not those who think they are righteous, but those who know they are sinners."

—Mark 2:16-18

In the neighborhood where I grew up, our gang of kids spent most of our free time outdoors in creative play. Our parents made sure of it! They set limits and boundaries and expected us to stay within them. We were free to roam within those boundaries as long as we showed respect for our neighbors and obeyed the rules. Yet even staying on my own fairly secure block, I could still cross "boundaries" and get hurt. I remember a chilly autumn day when I was six years old. We were all ramming about my friend's backyard. We had been warned to stay away from the swing set whenever anyone was swinging. I was playing an exciting game of tag and I forgot that rule. I ran straight into the path of the upward swinging glider. Before I knew what hit me I was laying on the ground with a large, profusely bleeding gash on my forehead. My mother, a registered nurse, proclaimed "This will need stitches." The dreaded "S" word! Mom said it would be okay and I held on tight.

Dr. Stroy met us at the emergency room. (His name often sounded like "Destroy!" to me.) He had me lie down on a table. His initial smile and gentle voice were reassuring. However, his bushy eyebrows furrowed as he inspected my wound. "Yes, stitches," he agreed softly. My mother stood by as "Dr. Destroy" and his nurse prepared to sew me up. I was okay until he bent over me to bring the pain numbing needle closer and closer to my eye. I began to whine and flail about.

Suddenly his voice changed into a sharp command, "Now listen here young man, you have a choice. You can be still and I can take care of you and have you on your way home soon or you can keep wiggling and crying and you might cause me to slip and poke your eye out! What will it be?" I was still, very still! Soon he was done and said, "Thank you son, you were very brave, I'm proud of you." What a relief! I don't know how brave I was, but I was certainly obedient under the old needle-in-the-eye threat!

Often times, clear warning about sharp consequences from a voice of authority is exactly what we need. The Lord is the Great Physician who wants us to trust and obey when He is working on our lives, relationships, souls, and bodies. But He also wants to teach us "preventive medicine" so we don't injure ourselves or others in the first place!

If Jesus is your Lord then the Holy Spirit guides you. Through Scripture, wise counsel, and His inner witness within you, He sets clear boundaries for your behavior. Within those boundaries you have His limited permission to move about and enjoy all His blessings. He wants you to seek His permission on any new endeavors or decisions because He knows what is best for you. He never wants you to go outside His boundaries. However, when He sees you trusting Him, He will expand your "neighborhood" and *lead* you into new adventures *with* Him! Along the way He wants to help you both resist temptation and boldly follow Him in your words and deeds.

Be still and know that I am God. Psalm 46:10

Real self-control means being still and letting God be God. You let the Spirit control your strengths and weaknesses. You truly let Jesus be your Lord and rest from running your own life.

Plastic self-control is prized in the world as self-discipline. This is as futile as the heavy yoke of self-confidence. Self-discipline means you attempt to control your strengths and weaknesses. Human history is replete with complete failure every time anyone has attempted to control anyone else. It doesn't work, not even when you try it on yourself.

The only One capable of controlling you for good is the One who made you, died for you, loves you—the One who *is* love. When humans attempt control then manipulation, oppression, and disaster are always the poisonous results.

Self-control means a God controlled self. The world has a distorted definition of control. "Control" does not mean to "dominate" or "manipulate." God's definition of control is "influence" which literally means to flow from within you!

Real self-control begins and ends with the Spirit who invites, warns, sorrows, convicts, cleanses, and invites again! The Holy Spirit wells up within always inviting you to walk closely with Him; warning if you are straying too close to crossing the line of sin; sorrowing within you if you cross the line; convicting you with real guilt to call you back across the line to receive forgiveness and cleansing; inviting you again to walk close to Him. What encouragement!

The plastic fruit of self-discipline begins and ends with your prideful self. You try hard to be a good person on your own power and values; eventually succumb to some temptation; feel the weight of shame and self-loathing; find someone or some thought to justify your actions; blame it on someone or something else; repress the memory; and move on less confident. It's a lonely existence of prideful striving, succumbing, shame, blame, repression, and wounded pride. Self-discipline becomes self-perpetuating self-defeat.

Pride precedes disaster, and an arrogant attitude precedes a fall. Proverbs 16:19 God's Word Translation

Five years after those first stitches, on a very hot humid summer day, my little brother and I decided to race our bikes down the block. We both boasted imminent victory. He had to stay on the sidewalk. I could ride in the street and would give him a big head start on his little twenty-inch bike with butterfly handlebars. "On your marks, set, go!" I waited until he reached his head start point and then I took off. My big single gear Western Flyer began to gain ground until I finally passed him well before the finish line. I stood up on my bike coasting at top speed and looked back laughing and taunting him when he yelled, "Look out!" It was too late. I turned to look and immediately crashed into the back of Mrs. Manchester's green Volkswagen beetle. Boom! My front tire hit the back bumper and I was launched like a missile into the car face first. More precisely, chin first. It gave new meaning to the term "slug bug." I slumped off the car onto the pavement with blood pouring from my chin. My brother helped me to the sidewalk and went to get Mrs. Manchester. She came and helped me into her house. Now, in the summer of 1968, Mrs. Manchester was the first person on our block to have central air conditioning. When I, no doubt in shock, hit that cold air I was faint for the first time in my life. So much for macho spoils of victory! My taunting was rewarded with, you guessed it, stitches. When I grow my winter beard no hair will grow through the scar under my chinny-chin-chin, a frosty reminder of a steamy summer lesson.

Touching old scars can help us remember and refrain from making the same arrogant mistake again. Oftentimes, we learn and grow in the fruit of the Spirit the hard way. Real self-control is also when the Spirit wells up to release memory and wisdom from old scars and you choose to follow His prompting onto the right path this time.

Competition in and of itself is not evil. However, pride leads with the chin and draws everyone around us into unnecessary pain and temptation to prideful responses. Pride lifts you up only to fall on your face. Humility lifts up others and steadies your legs. Pride taunts the loser and forfeits respect. Humility celebrates your competitor and gains a friend.

The sports entertainment industry is one forum of modern idolatry. I still enjoy rooting for my favorite teams and players while watching a good NFL game on TV. However, more and more I feel the restraining sorrow of the Holy Spirit for how prideful prancing and taunting is infecting athletes and fans from little league to the pros. This only reflects and perpetuates the famine of love. Yet it is so moving to see the few believer athletes who obviously follow the Spirit's influence. He is never without a witness! Certainly the Lord wants us to have good clean fun that builds people up. A Spirit led player gets to jump up and down in celebration of a touchdown, yet quickly returns to the sidelines in respect for everyone else. A Spirit led player in the midst of a series of plays will quickly go back to the huddle for the next play. Real self-control is to gratefully acknowledge applause by tipping one's cap or helmet to the crowd on the sideline.

The same goes for daily life. It's real humility to accept a compliment as a gift by saying a sincere thank you. It's false humility to deflect the compliment or to feed off it. It's not love to prance, taunt, or thrive off of human defeat or adulation. The Bible calls this "fear of man" and says that it is a snare.

Left to ourselves we will sooner or later be driven to act at the expense of others and press down upon them. Surrendering constant control to the Spirit we will more and more be led to act to the benefit of others and lift them up. Young shepherd David confronted a taunting spirit in the Philistine giant Goliath and brought him down under the trusted influence of the Spirit. Isaac had to re-dig old wells of his father Abraham which were filled in contemptuously by the taunting Philistines.

Self-control is last on the list of fruit of the Spirit. That's because real love's aim is a Spirit led life. The Lord loves you as you are but constantly hopes to influence you to become all you were made to be—His beloved Spirit led child. Real love to stitch up real wounds. Real influence to bring real freedom to roam with Him forever!

Chapter 30

Listen to Your Beloved

For all that is in the world—the lust of the flesh, the lust of the eyes, and the pride of life—is not of the Father but is of the world.

—1 John 2:16 NKJV

In late July of 1980, Kim and I took off on our honeymoon. Our destination was a little fisherman's cabin on a small lake in northern Minnesota. We were of modest means (weekly cabin rental was $95) yet lavish expectations! The best things in life are freely received. We traveled up Highway 52 into the twin cities of Minneapolis/St. Paul. Unfortunately, we hit the cities at rush hour. We were not accustomed to driving in a city that large. We were both stressed and there was no GPS in those days! Kim suggested we stop and ask directions but I insisted everything would be fine. All we had to do was look for the Highway 52 signs. We kept muddling along until we saw such a sign. We took that turn in temporary relief. However, soon Kim was uneasy again. Something wasn't right as she looked at the map. I said, "It doesn't matter what that map says, remember we both saw the Highway 52 sign, right?" She reluctantly agreed. We drove on. Several miles later she asked, "Do you think we should stop and ask directions?" My pride instantly kicked in, yet I retained my "honeymoon tone" and I politely declined. Several miles later she implored, "Sweetheart, I *really* think we need to stop and get directions!" I shook my head now throwing all newlywed caution to the wind and rudely pronounced, "All I know is I just saw a Highway 52 sign a few miles back, so I guarantee we are on the right road!" Kim paused several moments, then countered in a tone I would years later identify as "quiet victory." "Sweetheart," she began, "would you agree that the lake cabin is 100 miles *due north* of the twin cities?" I, not realizing I was a sheep being led to the slaughter, answered "Yes, of course!" To which she smiled with obvious glee and asked, "Then why have we been driving *directly west* into the sunset for over one hour???"

In the land of 10,000 lakes my pride died 10,000 deaths flaming out in the radiant orange Minnesota sunset. I apologized. We laughed. I apologized some more. We belly laughed louder. Then, for the first of many times in married life, we stopped and asked for directions. What a concept! At the gas station a kind, chuckling woman stated I had taken us out of the way and there was no easy shortcut back. That summer, *new* Highway 52 had just been completed and rerouted. But the signs of *old* Highway 52 had not yet been taken down! I had let my pride detour our blissful journey such that we would arrive several hours late in the pitch dark.

Pride is the enemy of self-control. Real self-control means the Lord is in the driver's seat. You are off the throne. You stop listening to your prideful will and listen only to His voice. You stop listening to the world's chatter and listen to the Only One who really knows how to live. Real self-control is you allowing your Beloved to truly lead your life.

My sheep hear my voice, and I know them, and they follow me. John 10:28 ESV

If you have truly received and confessed Jesus as your Lord and Savior, then He lives in you through the Holy Spirit. You have two voices in you. The voice that always tells you what the Bible says is Him. The voice that always tells you what you want to do is you! Self-control means your voice deferring to His. Jesus speaks to you clearly and simply through the Holy Spirit in you. At all times He is looking out for you. When you ask Him a question He will answer you with words or pictures forming in your mind that are in line with Bible truth that applies to your situation. He always speaks with the real fruit. In other words, if you are about to rush ahead of Him He will warn you in a way that works for you. For me, it's like little pink or red flags start waving in my mind. Pink means slow down. Red means stop. If He wants to let me know He is moving powerfully in my midst He will give me the feeling and image of being washed in a waterfall. If He wants to alert me to the presence of evil moving around me He will give me a stirring sense of an inner alarm to get up and pray or sing praise to drive the evil away.

Some people discount and ridicule "goose bumps." Others might make too much of it. The fact is the Holy Spirit does communicate with you from within your spirit, soul, and body. My wife will receive a burning sensation on her tongue and lower lip anytime the Holy Spirit is on the move around her. Therefore, when you receive a physical sensation like "goose bumps" open your heart and ask the Lord what it means. He will show you how this may relate to some aspect of His loving control. The Lord is supernatural in our natural bodies and there is a love famine because too many people are afraid to explore the depths of the sensitive leading of the Spirit.

Recently, we sought and received the Spirit's permission to buy a new laptop. We both prayed and I sensed an inner "Yes, go ahead" while Kim experienced confirming inner peace. We put the two together and decided to make the purchase without fear. But when we had to decide whether or not to buy the service/accident protection plan we both prayed and both heard separately the Lord say the same thing in our hearts—"Trust me!" So we did not purchase the plan. We had peace to step forward without fear and with confidence that the Lord will always work things out for us. He will do the same for you. The Lord is the storehouse within including the whispering voice of the Holy Spirit. He wants you to make two life changing decisions today. First, decide to believe Jesus that you can hear His voice in your heart. Second, decide to trust that the Lord speaks to you in every word of Scripture you read.

All Scripture is inspired by God and is useful to teach us what is true and to make us realize what is wrong in our lives. It corrects us when we are wrong and teaches us to do what is right. God uses it to prepare and equip his people to do every good work. 2 Timothy 3:16-17

Reading Scripture with an open trusting heart is like digital tuning your soul into the "frequency" of the Lord's voice. Frequency creates frequency! The more time you regularly read Scripture the more easily you will discern His voice leading you with self-control in every area of your life. The Holy Spirit breathed every word of Scripture in Bible writers' hearts.

Therefore, the Bible plus the Holy Spirit in you are like your personal GPS audio/visual guidance system. You can expect to clearly hear His voice in your trusting heart and see Him moving with eyes of childlike faith in *any* situation if you regularly and deeply open yourself to His Word.

At that time Jesus prayed this prayer: "O Father, Lord of heaven and earth, thank you for hiding these things from those who think themselves wise and clever, and for revealing them to the childlike. Yes, Father, it pleased you to do it this way! My Father has entrusted everything to me. No one truly knows the Son except the Father, and no one truly knows the Father except the Son and those to whom the Son chooses to reveal him." Matthew 11:25-27

Jesus only reveals Himself to a childlike trusting heart—through the Holy Spirit. Let Him restore your childlike heart.

Listen to your Beloved. He never makes a wrong turn with your life.

Chapter 31

Stir It Up

Let us hold fast the confession of our hope without wavering, for he who promised is faithful. And let us consider how to stir up one another to love and good works, not neglecting to meet together, as is the habit of some, but encouraging one another, and all the more as you see the Day drawing near.

—Hebrews 10:23-25 ESV

Once on summer vacation with our small children we spent the day simply admiring the view amidst the sandy rolling hills, sagebrush, rock formations, and big lonesome skies near Scottsbluff, Nebraska. We found a side road where the cattle grazed very close to the road. Our five-year-old daughter Emily noticed the bright yellow ear tags on a cow especially close by and called out, "Mommy, Daddy look! That cow is for sale!" We had a good laugh. Yes, cattle are usually for sale. But those ear tags specifically aid in tracking and protecting the herd from theft and disease.

The fruit of self-control is the Holy Spirit's way of tracking and protecting the Lord's flock from temptation and disease. The fruit of self-control is last on the list on the nine fruit of the Spirit because everything else He does in your life, all the other fruit, is aimed at giving you a pure and healthy Spirit led life. The New Testament Greek word for self-control is the only one of the nine fruit of the Spirit which is specifically tied to one issue—victory over immorality. The Lord created Adam and Eve to be fruitful and multiply in love. They rebelled. So do we. The Lord made us for receiving and giving love, but too often people settle for lust, greed, and pride. Immoral thoughts, words, and actions of lust, greed, and pride fuel the famine of love.

For all that is in the world—the lust of the flesh, the lust of the eyes, and the pride of life—is not of the Father but is of the world. 1 John 2:16 NKJV

As I have said, real self-control is you letting the Spirit lead your words and actions in love. Plastic self-control, self-discipline, is you leading yourself. The lust of the flesh is when in our loneliness we try to kill our pain through physical pleasure. The lust of the eyes (greed) is when in our loneliness we try to kill our insecurity through acquiring possessions. Pride of life is when in our loneliness we try to kill our despair through controlling people and circumstances. Real love received and given with other Christians deeply heals inner loneliness which is the breeding ground of temptation. It is a function of pride to try to control your sinful desires with your own strength.

But among you there must not be even a hint of sexual immorality, or of any kind of impurity, or of greed, because these are improper for God's holy people. Ephesians 5:3 NIV

You can't solve deep loneliness alone! You need to be in a regular gathering of other kindred believers where you stir one another up with so much love that you don't have time or need to give into sin. Simply put, self-control is the stirring up of love that continually shuts off sin inside you and amongst believers around you. Self-control is letting Jesus constantly help you avoid doing harm and abound in doing good. As with all the other nine fruit, self-control only grows in you when you are in healthy relationship with other believers. On your own you just get in deeper and pride, greed, and lust kill the fruit of the Spirit. The Lord does not raise spoiled children. He will keep calling to you, yet allow you to freely choose lust, greed, and pride and their horrible consequences. The ways of the Big Three, Father, Son, and Holy Spirit are the only way to defeat the immoral threesome of lust, greed, and pride. Still, pride wants us to find our own way.

Thus says the LORD: "Stand by the roads, and look, and ask for the ancient paths, where the good way is; and walk in it, and find rest for your souls. But they said, 'We will not walk in it.' Jeremiah 6:16 NKJV

If you humble yourself and let Jesus take control, He will help you live in constant victory over lust, greed, and pride. That constant victory will end the famine of love *within* you so you can end it *around* you. If cattle ranchers use ear tags to track and protect cattle from rustlers and disease, the Good Shepherd has His time tested ways to help His people *help each other* to defeat sin and unleash healing power.

Is anyone among you suffering? Let him pray. Is anyone cheerful? Let him sing praise. Is anyone among you sick? Let him call for the elders of the church, and let them pray over him, anointing him with oil in the name of the Lord. And the prayer of faith will save the one who is sick, and the Lord will raise him up. And if he has committed sins, he will be forgiven. Therefore, confess your sins to one another and pray for one another, that you may be healed. The prayer of a righteous person has great power as it is working. Elijah was a man with a nature like ours, and he prayed fervently that it might not rain, and for three years and six months it did not rain on the earth. Then he prayed again, and heaven gave rain, and the earth bore its fruit. My brothers, if anyone among you wanders from the truth and someone brings him back, let him know that whoever brings back a sinner from his wandering will save his soul from death and will cover a multitude of sins. James 5:13-20 ESV

If you know of a church of believers who are meeting in small groups according to James 5 and Hebrews 10 please imitate them! The Lord is calling all believers back to the ancient paths of simple, deep, vigilant love in small groups truly focused on Christ. The Lord wants you to unite with other believers in a real fruit bearing small group. Lots of churches try all kinds of small groups gathered around topics and special interests, but if those groups do not focus in on James 5 and Hebrews 10 then there will be little real fruit. Two thousand years of history with the Holy Spirit shows time and again that He waits for believers to gather only around Christ as their focus and to practice the ancient paths.

As long as a small group is committed to the ancient paths of wholehearted praise, scriptural truth, prayer and fasting in faith, loving each other, sharing possessions, mutual accountability, and helping the poor—the Holy Spirit will produce bountiful fruit.

There are several different ways to configure authentic New Testament fruit bearing groups. Please don't get caught up in all the debate about such things. Stay focused. Keep it simple and real, true to the Scriptures.

Our house fellowship consists of believers from many different churches who meet in our home each Sunday night. We call the mixed group of men and women "I58 House Fellowship." We seek to be Spirit-led followers of Jesus who love each other while seeking divine appointments 24/7 to love people from the Lord's heart expressed in Isaiah chapter 58.

We ask the Lord to help us love people in our city and churches with no strings attached. We are committed to renewal and unity in the Body of Christ and helping the church get outside "the four walls." We are lay people and pastors from various traditions called to watch over each other in love. We seek to break down the barriers between lay people and pastors so that we all simply love one another as brothers and sisters. We are all called to preach the gospel every day and every where the Spirit leads us.

The word "preach" simply means to proclaim the gospel of Christ in our daily words and deeds. If a sermon bears the fruit of the Spirit then it is real preaching. But real preaching is much more than sermons. The fruit of the Spirit coming out of you in loving words and deeds is real "preaching!"

In our I58 House Meeting we gather each week for two hours as brothers and sisters to sing and pray to the Lord, let the Lord speak to our hearts in the Scriptures, break bread together, and give and receive real love with each other. Our house meetings are open to believers and not-yet believers, but we do not hold back from passionate worship, prayer, and teaching of truth in love. We often have thirty people seeking after God in our living and dining rooms. There was a day several years ago when we rarely opened our home. Never again. Real people everywhere with real needs need to experience real fruit.

We also have I-58 Covenant Groups which are smaller than the House Meeting. Each group is limited to five men believers or five women believers. We do not mix men and women together in these smallest groups. We believe this to be another healthy protection against any hint of immorality. These groups meet for one hour each week for love, accountability, and prayer. We each report on three questions:

1. How is it with your soul?
Confess your sins to one another... James 5:16—We report on any way in the last week we were tempted in lust, greed, or pride and how the Lord helped us escape it, or how we stumbled and were led to repentance.

2. How is the Holy Spirit prompting you to bear fruit like Jesus?
And let us consider how to stir up one another to love and good works. Hebrews 10:24—We report how the Lord is coaching us in Scripture, prayer, fasting, and wise counsel to love and witness to others. We are not to become inward focused, but to end the famine of love in our city.

3. How can we pray for you?
...and pray for each other and you will be healed. James 5:16—We take careful notes on each report and commit to pray for each one daily during the week. Then one person places their hand on the shoulder of the person to the right of them and prays aloud for them according to their report. We pray briefly, yet deeply, with love and faith as we go around the circle until finished. The reports and prayers are easily accomplished in less than one hour. We spend any remaining time thanking the Lord.

We all make covenant to meet weekly for three to six months. Each person agrees to make that meeting a priority. At the end of that time, we remix the groups with different members for the next three to six months. We do this to avoid becoming ingrown and also for love to deepen across the fellowship. The accumulative effect of such regular meeting is ever deepening faith, hope, and love. We are now seeing more and more miraculous answers to prayer by the day! The reason for so few healings and miracles is the neglect of such meetings in the Body of Christ. Real fruit comes from following His word. Any group of sincere believers in any church can do this. The Holy Spirit will help because it is according to His words.

These three historic questions from the Holy Spirit were employed by early Moravians and Wesleyans as they sought to live out Hebrews 10 and James 5 in small group life. They knew the stakes were high. The more we watch over each other in real love, the more pure hearted we become, the more bold and loving witnesses we become, the more the Holy Spirit moves to bring more lost souls into the Kingdom. When we neglect to meet regularly the fires go out as evidenced throughout history.

There is something unique about gathering in one another's homes. From the very beginning, the Holy Spirit has called Christ followers to gather regularly in large and small gatherings to bear real fruit.

And they devoted themselves to the apostles' teaching and the fellowship, to the breaking of bread and the prayers. And awe came upon every soul, and many wonders and signs were being done through the apostles. And all who believed were together and had all things in common. And they were selling their possessions and belongings and distributing the proceeds to all, as any had need. And day by day, attending the temple together and breaking bread in their homes, they received their food with glad and generous hearts, praising God and having favor with all the people. And the Lord added to their number day by day those who were being saved. Acts 2:42-47 ESV

Notice the Holy Spirit had the early believers gathering in a large group in the temple courts. Gathering together in a large group at a church sanctuary for worship can be very fruitful or not. We are glad to worship on Sunday morning in the large group congregation gathered in the sanctuary of the church we attend. A large setting bears real fruit when we all gather in unity for an audience of One. He deserves that! When the praise of Jesus is the primary focus, with the simple gospel of Christ faithfully proclaimed, and people welcomed with real love, then the Father will always dispatch the Holy Spirit to increase faith, hope, and love in the midst of a large gathering.

If these basic elements of worship are not present things get "plastic" in a hurry. It's not a question of music or liturgical style, but the wholehearted praise of Jesus and thanksgiving for His life, death, and resurrection. Wherever the person and work of Christ on the cross is the focus, there will be fruit. Anything less bears little. It does not matter the difference in doctrine or denomination, large or small group settings are no guarantee of real fruit unless Jesus is the center, lifted up with real faith, hope, and love. But large group worship services are not best suited for deepening relationships in real love in the body of Christ. The Lord's way for our roots to go deep is gathering together regularly in smaller groups in our homes.

Famine of love happens because we Christians often treat our homes as personal fortresses in which to hide privately from the harsh world instead of opening our homes to small gatherings of believers which become well-watered gardens bearing real fruit. When we open up our homes, He breaks fear off of us and we open our hearts even more deeply to Him and others. Even in strong, Bible believing churches there is often a deep disconnect between what people profess at church and the way they live at home. The more you welcome people into your home for prayer, praise, study, love, and accountability, the more your home life will be filled with the fruit of the Spirit. It's a lot harder to hide from the Lord when you keep inviting Him and His people into you into *your* "sanctuary."

When you begin to do this, you will find the Holy Spirit changing you from within and you will stop hiding from the love-starved people in your city or neighborhood. He will release in you His heart for hurting people. Then all you have to do is ask Him to give you opportunities every day to love someone out there and it will happen.

So what are you waiting for? You may not have room for thirty people in your home, but I bet you have room for five. Why am I so ardent about the necessity of small group life for bearing the fruit of self-control? Real Christianity is deeply personal, but not individualistic. When the Holy Spirit led Paul to write his letters he always emphasized that to be in Christ was always personal and corporate. You can't grow in Christ alone. That's not His way.

My wife Kim once took a jar filled with dark thick gunk to the sink and turned the faucet on. She watched as the constant overflow of water going into the jar eventually turned the contents from black, to gray to milky, to clear. She realized the Lord was showing her the way He wants people to get rid of their dirty lives. You decide to stop putting in more gunk and instead keep pouring in the good stuff. Yes, you need to lean on the Lord and stop all watching, reading, and listening to things that are lust, greed, and pride inspiring. Become an enemy of sin, particularly your own. Love the Lord and yourself enough to stop the bad input. Ask other Christian friends to pray for you and enter into accountable relationships with them. If you don't do that, you will not defeat sin in your life.

The best way to eliminate lust, greed, and pride from your life is to ask Jesus to fill you with the Holy Spirit to constantly overflowing. Ask for that daily. Fill up your heart with love for Jesus, fill up your home with people hungry to give and receive love, and help fill up your church with people who let Jesus love them and who love Him back with all their heart—and the Holy Spirit will continually draw hurting people into your path.

Simply put, self-control is letting Jesus lead you to constantly avoid doing harm and abounding in doing good. You can't do it alone. You can always do it with a little regular help from His friends.

If we all keep stirring up the good stuff we'll have no time to stir up the bad stuff. You and I have been tagged, chosen, appointed to bear fruit. People are not cattle or sheep. People all around you are living with sin and shame that is out of control. They need to be loved by people full of self-control and the healing power of Jesus. Let's be those people.

Don't allow love to turn into lust, setting off a downhill slide into sexual promiscuity, filthy practices, or bullying greed. Though some tongues just love the taste of gossip, those who follow Jesus have better uses for language than that. Don't talk dirty or silly. That kind of talk doesn't fit our style. Thanksgiving is our dialect. Ephesians 5:3-4, The Message

Let's pray:

Lord Jesus, I lay down my burdens of lust, greed, and pride at Your feet. I am Your beloved child. Help me make the necessary changes to walk closer with You and with my brothers and sisters in healthy mission for You! Amen.

THE ADVENTURE AHEAD

Chapter 32

A Wonderful Adventure

Finally brethren, whatever is true, whatever is noble, whatever is just, whatever is pure, whatever is lovely, whatever is of good report, if there be anything of virtue, if anything is praiseworthy—meditate on these things.

—Philippians 4:8 NKJV

My favorite poet, Robert Frost, once stopped to ponder divergent paths through an autumn forest. He chose the path less traveled and found it made all the difference.

Pause and consider your path ahead. The Lord loves you completely. A new heaven and a new earth are coming with His return. Only He knows when. Only He knows the path He wants you to travel until that great day.

Several years ago Kim and I faced a crossroads. We were certain the Lord wanted us to spend our lives inviting people to come rest in His love. There were two legitimate paths. One was the familiar security of leading a congregation while writing books and leading retreats and outreaches in our spare time. We would have steady financial provision but less time to do what was burning in our hearts. The other path meant leaving salary and benefits for maximum freedom to write and spread our message wherever the Spirit would lead *and* provide. It was a little scary.

I went into the quiet church sanctuary one afternoon and cried out, "Lord help me know the way to go!" After I grew quiet a thought came spoken with gusto. "I have a wonderful adventure ahead for you and Kim!" *Wonderful adventure.* Peace came. I sensed His heart was giddy with anticipation! I saw us traversing together with Him over mountains with all the twists and turns of a roller coaster. Fear evaporated in rising joy. It was time to step away from the familiar.

At our farewell, we were presented a quilt upon which many friends wrote loving words. In one quilt block a pastor colleague wrote, "Blessings as you have now chosen the road less traveled."

The Lord Himself is the road less traveled. He wants to be trusted completely. I now see He called us to this particular adventure because it was His most loving path for Kim and me. For someone else, His path may have been to stay in the traditional church.

You don't have anything to prove to anyone. The only thing you need to do is let Him love you and lead you. He never fails. He knows you, He loves you, and He has your best interest at heart.

Robert Tuttle once told me, "The Lord has more invested in your life, your loved ones, your ministry, than you do. You can trust Him." The Lord will make things abundantly clear when you need to step forward and will increase your faith when you need to wait where you are. As long as you seek after Him, He will always give you what you need in the adventure.

For God is working in you, giving you the desire and the power to do what pleases him. Philippians 2:13

Seek His peace and permission for what He has given you great desire to do. He will give you the green light to proceed unless He sees something harmful you might not yet see. As you wait in stillness, trust afresh that He *is* the path less traveled. He makes all the difference.

Enter by the narrow gate; for wide is the gate and broad is the way that leads to destruction, and there are many who go in by it. Because narrow is the gate and difficult is the way which leads to life, and there are few who find it. "Beware of false prophets, who come to you in sheep's clothing, but inwardly they are ravenous wolves. You will know them by their fruits. Do men gather grapes from thornbushes or figs from thistles? Even so, every good tree bears good fruit, but a bad tree bears bad fruit. Matthew 7:13-18 NKJV

How can you tell the difference between the well worn path of bad fruit and the less traveled path of good fruit?

The narrow road of real fruit is often more difficult, the way of the cross. Yet His path is always a wonderful adventure that ends in resurrection.

The well worn way is the path of least resistance, the short cut, the most convenient, the instantly gratifying, the least hassle, the least convicting, the least sacrificial, the laziest, the cheapest, the stingiest, the most manipulative, the most fear-motivated, the most oppressive, the most destructive. This path ends in famine.

In early America, pathfinders would light torches, mark trees, or pile rocks as signs for pioneers to follow. In every circumstance look for the eight "torches" of Philippians 4:8. He can show you these things at all times because He is holding all things together *and* because He lives in you looking out at your world.

Whenever you decide to stop and look for these markers the Holy Spirit will steadily clear away the gunk to help you see His way to go. There is nothing that is truly one of these eight that is not *of* Him and *from* Him. When you trace back the source of every truly worthwhile thing in life it all comes back to Christ.

In this new life, it doesn't matter if you are a Jew or a Gentile, circumcised or uncircumcised, barbaric, uncivilized, slave, or free. Christ is all that matters, and he lives in all of us. Colossians 3:11

Try it now. Slow down, stop, and meditate. Consider how the Risen Christ is each one of these eight things *right now.* He isn't a dead figure from the past. He is with you so choose to *be with* Him by meditating upon Him. Paul, the writer of Philippians 4:8, knew and preached a living Risen Lord who had confronted him on the road to Damascus when he was persecuting Christians.

For I decided to know nothing among you except Jesus Christ and him crucified. 1 Corinthians 2:2 ESV

Paul did not know Jesus before He was crucified. He only knew the living Christ who chose to be crucified for him and the whole world. Christ and His work on the cross was all Paul ever wanted to know, preach, and live. Christ and His work on the cross was the lens through which Paul learned to view every person, circumstance, and decision. When you view everything in light of the crucified living Christ then you are actually grounding yourself in *reality!* You are putting yourself in position to be led by the Spirit.

Christ and His work on the cross *is* all that really matters for your past, present, and future.

If you don't meditate on Christ you can drift until you are thinking and acting as if there is no crucified Christ to fill you and lead you with His love. When we think and act as if Christ is not alive then we are in a pitiable place.

And if Christ has not been raised, your faith is futile and you are still in your sins... If in Christ we have hope in this life only, we are of all people most to be pitied. But in fact Christ has been raised from the dead, the firstfruits of those who have fallen asleep. 1 Corinthians 15:17-20 ESV

If you don't really believe He is with you, how can you choose to receive and give His love? If you don't feast on Him you begin to starve right along with everyone else. But once you really receive Him in your heart, He really lives in you! And even though you may choose to not focus on Him, He does not stop focusing on you. You are always on His mind.

Nicole C. Mullen recorded "Redeemer" a few years ago and I can never listen to the song without tears of joy. The core of my being knows my Redeemer lives. He died on the cross, rose from the grave, sent the Holy Spirit into my life, saved me, and called me to spread His love. Though I am weak, forgetful, and still stumble, He is my loving Daddy, Lord, and Friend all wrapped up into One who is always with me, always loving me.

If you don't yet trust and love Jesus, He is knocking on the door of your heart asking for you to finally say "Yes."

If you already trust and love Jesus, then *you know deep down* this is all true because His Spirit is in you saying "Yes." If you start acting as if He is not in you He will begin prompting you with thoughts to turn to him. If you burden yourself with sin, you will know it's wrong because the Holy Spirit is lovingly convicting you from within. If you keep straying you will feel increasingly sad because the Holy Spirit within you is grieving because you are hurting Him and hurting yourself and others around you.

As you look at your path ahead you have a choice, deprivation or dedication. Will you deprive the Lord, yourself, and others of what could be your Spirit led life? Or will you dedicate yourself to the One who has dedicated Himself for your everlasting welfare?

Your dedicated path with Him may be less traveled and more difficult but it will always be illuminated by the Holy Spirit through the eight "torches" of Philippians 4:8. Rest assured, your journey ahead will be a great adventure all the way to your eternal home. He will see to it that you see His path as you meditate upon the "great eight."

Learn to practice daily what Paul preaches. Ask the Holy Spirit to help you and soon you will think more like Him at all times and real fruit will come forth. Basically, you think about each of these eight great things about Him *and* the same attribute you see in yourself and others.

True is the way things really are from His perspective.
Noble is the high road of self-sacrifice.
Just is standing Christlike against evil.
Pure is wholehearted desire for Christlikeness.
Lovely is the beauty of no-strings attached love.
Good Report is only speaking of others' godly qualities.
Virtue is pursuit of excellence without oppressing others.
Praiseworthy is thinking and acting like Christ.

The chart below could aid you in your reflection.

THE GREAT EIGHT TORCHES

	Christ	Myself	Others
True			
Noble			
Just			
Pure			
Lovely			
Good Report			
Virtue			
Praiseworthy			

Set aside ten minutes a day. Sit in a quiet place with pen and your Great Eight Torches chart. Ask the Lord to show you each of the great eight about Him, you, and others. Watch what happens. For example, think about whatever is true about Christ. For example, you might say, "Jesus, You are Lord over all creation!" Ponder that a moment.

Next, consider what is true about you from His perspective. The Holy Spirit will bring some thought or picture to your mind to encourage you. You might say, "Lord, I am your beloved child. You will never forsake me." Rest a moment in His love. See what comes from Him.

Then, consider what is true about others of your family, friends, acquaintances, or enemies. Ask the Lord to show you what is true about them from His perspective. He will! You might say, "Lord, You love ____ completely and gave Yourself on the cross for him/her!"

Repeat these statements of real truth about Christ, yourself, and others. Focus on each word. Write them down. Declare them throughout your day. The Holy Spirit will bring more good thoughts and give you more of Jesus' heart for the people in your life. It will change the way you treat them, it will change you!

Repeat this process with each of the great eight attributes. As you practice this you will become more attuned to who Christ is and where He wants to lead you. If you have to decide between two paths, there will clearly be more of the great eight torches favoring one of the paths. That is the way He wants you to go.

I will never forget how the Lord lifted my heart, my eyes with two words—*wonderful adventure.* He painted a *lovely* picture of a path less traveled and that has made all the difference.

He has a wonderful adventure ahead for you. Not someone else's path, but His path for you. What path ahead has the most "great eight torches"? That's the path upon which your life will bear the most of the nine real fruit of the Spirit.

Come follow your wonderful Savior on the adventure of a lifetime! Come end the famine of love.

Let's pray:

Lord Jesus, I repent of fixing my mind on things that dishonor You and disable me. Please forgive me, flush my mind, and heal me of all unrighteousness. Help me make the good choices to fill my mind with Your good stuff that my heart will be pure and so sensitive to the whisper of Your voice, the brush of Your hand. I do want to follow You wherever You want to lead me. I love you with all my heart. Amen.

Chapter 33

Destination Jesus

Thomas said, "Master, we have no idea where you're going. How do you expect us to know the road?" Jesus said, I am the Road, also the Truth, also the Life. No one gets to the Father apart from me. If you really knew me, you would know my Father as well. From Jesus now on, you do know him. You've even seen him!"

—John 14:5-7, The Message

On that same vacation drive through the back roads of western Nebraska, our three-year-old son was becoming impatient. While we took in the natural beauty, Daniel spoke up from the back seat, "When are we going to get there?" His mother patiently responded, "Honey, we're not really going *to* any place, we're just driving to look at things." He repeated his question and was given the same answer a number of times. Finally Daniel asked one last time, "When are we going to get there?" Before his mom could respond, he quickly rolled his eyes and answered himself, "Oh, I know, we're not going *any*place!"

The Lord has His own plan for the future and can often seem slow and to take us on too many off roads. It would please our flesh if He would give us His roadmap and schedule. But that's not His way to a truly fruitful life.

In Jesus' three years leading the first disciples most of the significant things He did happened "along the way" in between stops. The best the world has to offer you is a goal driven life. It's not a bad thing. However, Jesus does not offer you goals and strategy to get you through life. He offers you Himself.

The disciples said, "We do not know the way you are going, show us the way.' Jesus answered them, "I am the Way, and the Truth, and the Life. No one comes to the Father, except by Me." John 14:6

The disciples were looking for a different answer. He was looking for the right time to die. They were preparing for victory over Rome. He was preparing them for His victory over death. His ways were not their ways. They could not comprehend that *He* is the roadmap, *He* is the destination. All history is ultimately about Him. If you want to get where you really need to go, following Christ is all that matters.

Put on your new nature, and be renewed as you learn to know your Creator and become like him. In this new life, it doesn't matter if you are a Jew or a Gentile, circumcised or uncircumcised, barbaric, uncivilized, slave, or free. Christ is all that matters, and he lives in all of us. Colossians 3:10-11

What really matters for eternity will be decided around Jesus and His love. If you are ever confused or discouraged in the adventure ahead, the place to begin is Him. He will get you through to the other side which is… Him!

On the same day, when evening had come, He said to them, "Let us cross over to the other side." And a great windstorm arose, and the waves beat into the boat, so that it was already filling. But He was in the stern, asleep on a pillow. And they awoke Him and said to Him, "Teacher, do You not care that we are perishing?" Then He arose and rebuked the wind, and said to the sea, "Peace, be still!" And the wind ceased and there was a great calm. But He said to them, "Why are you so fearful? How is it that you have no faith?" Mark 4:35, 37-40 NKJV

A frightening storm arose in the middle of the lake. Jesus is sleeping secure in the back of the boat with his head on a cushion. The boat is filling up with water. I always see a hilarious picture of water lapping up against his cheek! But it wasn't hilarious to the disciples. The frightened cries of His friends awaken the Lord, something the storm couldn't do. They come to the desperate point fearing He didn't care about them. Have you ever felt like that? He awakes and calms the storm and then asks them why they are so afraid. Had they forgotten what He said before they got in the boat? "Let's go to the other side." Think about it. Jesus himself asks you to go with Him on a journey to the other side. Jesus himself is in the boat with you the whole time. What is there to fear?

If you have given your life to Christ, He has promised to get you to where He wants to take you. Along the way there will be storms but just remember all that matters is Christ in you.

Recently during our I58 group we were considering the storm story in Mark 4. Kim had a little playful song "ditty" come to her and she led us in a hilarious faith rendition. Picture thirty adults waving their arms, tapping their toes, and giggling as they sing in a country western twang reminiscent of the old TV show *Hee Haw*.

"Ohhhh,

we ain't gonna sink in the middle of the lake

We ain't gonna sink in the middle of the lake

We ain't gonna sink in the middle of the laaaaake…

'Cause we're goin' to the other side

We're goin' to the other side

We're goin' to the other side

We ain't gonna sink in the middle of the laaaaaake…

'Cause we're goin' to the other siiiiiide!"

It might not sound too religious, but the Holy Spirit increased our faith and hope in the midst of a whole lot of laughter, clapping, and love!

Right now we are all somewhere in the "middle of the lake." Only the Lord knows how close we are to the other side. The Holy Spirit's unfinished business is to prepare the Bride, all true believers, to grow in His fruit radiant with holiness and godliness until that Day. The family of believers worldwide still has much "spot and blemish" —unholiness and ungodliness and He still wants to bring many more into the fold.

…with the Lord one day is as a thousand years, and a thousand years as one day. The Lord is not slow to fulfill his promise as some count slowness, but is patient toward you, not wishing that any should perish, but that all should reach repentance. But the day of the Lord will come like a thief, and then the heavens will pass away with a roar… Since all these things are thus to be dissolved, what sort of people ought you to be in lives of holiness and godliness… waiting for new heavens and a new earth in which righteousness dwells. Therefore… be

diligent to be found by him without spot or blemish, and at peace. 2 Peter 3:8-14 ESV

To be "holy" means to be pure hearted toward the Lord. To be "godly" means to be fruitful toward people. This is how He wants you to live in the adventure ahead.

The world is speeding toward that day of His choosing. There are many good and terrible times ahead. Only those who will come rest in His loving arms will not lose heart. Jesus told us these stormy days would come.

Just before He returns there will be little famine of love in the church, and because of this many more people will be drawn to Jesus. But right now the Bride is quite often more focused upon herself than the Lord. We are often more concerned about budgets, buildings, and programs rather than simple pure hearted love for Jesus and neighbor. Yet the Lord is so patient with His bride! He is moving to deeply awaken love in us. He is whispering to more and more believers this simple calling, "Gather in large groups to passionately love Me; gather in small groups to deeply love one another; and bear My fruit in the world witnessing in Spirit-led words and deeds."

Until one has tasted real fruit it's easy to settle for plastic. Once we taste the real we won't settle for less. The real fruit of the Spirit never stops growing because the moment it bursts with flavor and nutrients from you toward someone, the Holy Spirit's powerful seeds begin growing in their life. So ends the famine of love. As you continue to eat and share real fruit with others you will be awakened and set ablaze with His love. As people notice your fire, many will respond with joy. But just as some rejected Jesus, some will also reject Jesus *in* you.

Let Him work His unfinished business in you. He has appointed you to be pure hearted toward Him and bear real fruit toward people. Rid your life of impurity and rest from plastic activity.

Time is short. His love is not. He is making His last call to the earth before His return, "Come to Me all who are weary and heavy laden and I will give you rest." Come rest and bear His best.

No matter the storms, we won't sink in the middle of the lake. He's taking us to the other side.

When are we going to get there? That's up to Him. Until then let's enjoy the ride—increasingly pure hearted and fruitful.

Chapter 34

Wellsprings, Buckets, and Seeds

The Lord will guide you continually, giving you water when you are dry and restoring your strength. You will be like a well-watered garden, like an ever-flowing spring.

—Isaiah 58:11

A few years ago, the Lord brought a picture to my mind. I believe it is a glimpse of what's ahead. I see wellsprings, buckets, and seeds. Storm clouds will gather, yet the Holy Spirit will prepare the Bride for the Bridegroom's return.

I see geysers like Old Faithful (representing the Lord's real presence) welling up from Christians gathering in real love. I then see buckets (true Christ centered outreach groups bearing real fruit) jettisoned out of these geysers arching all over the earth and wherever they land disappear like seeds into the ground. Immediately more geysers erupt, buckets jettison, seeds penetrate and the process perpetuates until the Lord returns.

Unprecedented evil will be answered by the unprecedented real presence of the Lord and real fruit of His people. No matter the hellish persecution, the victory shout of the Lord's people will grow louder. The joy of the Lord will be our strength, the Lord's storehouse within believers will be released in relentlessly advancing oases, and millions of love-starved people will come into Jesus' arms.

May it ever be so for you, me, and the people around us in expanding circles of the well-watered gardens of the Lord.

Be loved, beloved.

You did not choose me, but I chose you and appointed you so that you might go and bear fruit—fruit that will last—and so that whatever you ask in my name the Father will give you. This is my command: Love each other. John 15:16-17 NIV

Reflection/ Discussion Questions

The purpose of this book is to help you open up and surrender more deeply to the Lord. This is not really a "how to" book, it is a "come to" book. The questions are merely suggestions. You won't have something come to mind about every question. The questions are just to help you open up to more intimacy and conversation with the Lord.

If you are using this book as a group study, you will have the best discussion experience if you make it a personal sharing and testimony time. When your group gathers have someone read a chapter aloud, and then ask people to share anything they would like relative to the reflection questions. Suggest that people don't have to share, they get to share if they choose. Once sharing and questions cease, go on to the next chapter. This will provide a gentle spiritual focus. When you jump into discussion without reading the chapter aloud, you might miss out on all the Holy Spirit wants to do in the session. Don't rush but let the Holy Spirit keep your discussion *openhearted*. When people stop sharing or begin to debate or philosophize, it's time to move on. Group sessions should focus on how Jesus is inviting each person to a closer walk with Him.

Introduction

Feast or Famine

1. What do you like about this chapter?
2. What feelings, memories, or questions arise?
3. Have you ever skinned your knee big time? Who helped you?
4. Who has loved on you in the last seventy-two hours? Thank Him!
5. Who have you loved on in the last seventy-two hours? Thank Him!
6. Where do you see famine of love around you?
7. What do you seek from the Lord in this book?

Invitation

1 Your Unguarded Heart

1. What do you like about this chapter?
2. What feelings, memories, or questions arise?
3. Have you ever been around a silo or a sand dune?
4. How are you guarding your heart from evil?
5. How are you letting down your guard to Jesus?
6. What wounds or walls must you surrender?
7. What do you desire most in coming years? Ask!

2 Silos and Sand Dunes

1. What do you like about this chapter?
2. What feelings, memories, or questions arise?
3. Name three ways the fruit of the Spirit are manifest.
4. Which one of the nine fruit is most evident in you?

5. Which one of the nine fruit is most lacking in you?
6. Which one of the nine fruit do you need most now?

3 A Contest Of Wills

1. What do you like about this chapter?
2. What feelings, memories, or questions arise?
3. Just how much do you like chocolate?
4. Do you remember pushing your parents too far?
5. Are you going to Jesus or just going to church?
6. What ten Isaiah 58 actions show living for Him?
7. What fifteen rotten fruit come from our sin nature?
8. How do you need to yield control to the Lord?

4 Well-Watered

1. What do you like about this chapter?
2. What feelings, memories, or questions arise?
3. Have you ever had, or dug, a well?
4. What does quarreling require?
5. How is He helping you dig out the "gunk?"
6. What rebellion or quarreling must you dig out?
7. What is a next step to be an "oasis" to people close to you?

Real Love

5 Accept No Substitutes

1. What do you like about this chapter?
2. What feelings, memories, or questions arise?
3. What did you enjoy collecting as a kid?
4. How are you settling for less than God's best?
5. What cheap substitutes must go from your life?
6. How has He given you grace after blowing it?
7. What people near you need grace from you?

6 Freely And Lightly

1. What do you like about this chapter?
2. What feelings, memories, or questions arise?
3. Ever have an old rag shirt or the equivalent?
4. Of what does the Lord want you to let go?
5. What or Who are you gripping in life?
6. Are any strings attached in your relationships?
7. Is the Lord your one true treasure?
8. How is He freeing you to love & enjoy people ?

7 Rest-oration

1. What do you like about this chapter?
2. What feelings, memories, or questions arise?
3. Have you invited Jesus to, "Make Himself at home?"
4. How are you using, not loving, people?
5. Where do you see mutual self-interest, not love?
6. Do you love all people in your church?
7. Do you rent, or love your pastor?
8. How do you need to speak less and love more?

Real Joy

8 What A Ride

1. What do you like about this chapter?
2. What feelings, memories, or questions arise?
3. Have you ever been brightened by a free spirit?
4. How does your mood depend on newscasts?
5. How are you depending on His Good News?
6. Do people brighten when you show up?

9 Victory Shout

1. What do you like about this chapter?
2. What feelings, memories, or questions arise?
3. What was a fun victory you witnessed?
4. What is the "joy of the Lord?"
5. What is "rejoicing?"
6. When did you last shout your praise of Jesus?
7. When is the next time you shout your praise?

10 Hang Time

1. What do you like about this chapter?
2. What feelings, memories, or questions arise?
3. What does it mean to you to be a best friend?
4. What was a thrilling worship time for you?
5. What are Jesus' three steps in abiding in John 15:7?
6. How do you spell "love?"
7. What is His time tested way in Psalm 5?
8. What two things inhibit constant companionship?
9. What's your plan for more alone time with Him? (Feel free to jump ahead to chapter 25)

Real Peace

11 Difference Maker

1. What do you like about this chapter?
2. What feelings, memories, or questions arise?
3. Who was your wisest teacher or coach and why?
4. Who needs some reassurance through you?
5. Who needs parental guidance through you?
6. Are you letting Him help you with secret sins?
7. How are you following the Ten Commandments?

12 Take Heart

1. What do you like about this chapter?
2. What feelings, memories, or questions arise?
3. What's your favorite book or movie? Why?
4. What does "taking heart" simply mean?
5. Why does He have you reading this chapter right now?
6. Are you a person of peace? Why? Why not?

13 Warrior Prince

1. What do you like about this chapter?
2. What feelings, memories, or questions arise?
3. Has Jesus ever ticked you off? How did you respond?
4. How do Jesus' words slice you away from evil?
5. How is His truth replacing your opinions?
6. What are your vain pursuits of "peace of mind?"
7. What people near you need real peace?
8. What does the Lord want you to do next?

Real Patience

14 Taking Care Of Business

1. What do you like about this chapter?
2. What feelings, memories, or questions arise?
3. Have you heard of Bachman Turner Overdrive?
4. Have you ever bullied or been bullied?
5. What is false patience?
6. How is the Lord helping you wait on Him?
7. Who is bullying or being bullied around you?
8. What does the Lord want you to do about it?

15 The Thief's Promise

1. What do you like about this chapter?
2. What feelings, memories, or questions arise?
3. Have you ever run outside in your underwear!?
4. What makes you react in fear?
5. How are you learning to respond in love?
6. Do you dread or welcome the Lord's return?

16 The Longest Fuse

1. What do you like about this chapter?
2. What feelings, memories, or questions arise?
3. Have you ever been a bonehead?
4. What people have "short fuses" around you?
5. What is righteous anger?
6. Do you have anger now? What kind?
7. How has the Lord been patient with you?
8. Who do you need His patience for? Pray.

Real Kindness

17 Unexpected Mercy

1. What do you like about this chapter?
2. What feelings, memories, or questions arise?
3. Are you aging playfully kind, or grumpy?
4. What differs between fake and real kindness?
5. Do you listen for others' mistakes or their pain?
6. How has the Lord given you unexpected mercy?
7. Do you look at yourself the way the Lord does?
8. Who once stopped to help you instead of passing by?
9. Who is "lying upon the road bleeding" near you?

18 Easy Does It

1. What do you like about this chapter?
2. What feelings, memories, or questions arise?
3. Who gave you real mercy when you were young?
4. What is real kindness?
5. Have you been placing burdens or lifting burdens lately?
6. How has Jesus lifted your burdens?
7. How do you need to draw closer "to his thigh?"
8. Will you ask for the Lord's heart for all people?

19 Healing Hands Warm Heart

1. What do you like about this chapter?
2. What feelings, memories, or questions arise?
3. What embarrassing fear do you want Him to Heal?
4. Do you want to "move mountains" in His name?
5. What doubts do you need to let go of?
6. What grudges do you need to let go of?
7. What other sin habits do need to let go of?
8. Do you want people healed in body and soul? Ask!
9. How bold and relentless will you pray?

Real Goodness

20 Free Stuff

1. What do you like about this chapter?
2. What feelings, memories, or questions arise?
3. When did you last giggle or belly laugh?
4. Who last poured out real goodness on you?
5. What is real giving?
6. Do you fearfully hoard or joyfully give?
7. Are there plastic "shoulds" that need to go?

8. Do you want to be like Barnabas? Ask!
9. Who needs radical generosity from you now?

21 Pause and Wonder

1. What do you like about this chapter?
2. What feelings, memories, or questions arise?
3. Do you take time to ponder in the Christmas season?
4. Do you pause & wonder at the end of each day?
5. Who are the generous people of your past?
6. How has the Lord been generous to you?

22 I Am Not Enough

1. What do you like about this chapter?
2. What feelings, memories, or questions arise?
3. When did you last really praise God in a park?
4. Who is deeply, permanently committed to you?
5. Who needs your deep permanent commitment?
6. When did the Lord last have to correct you?
7. Do you need His correction now?
8. Are you willing to be weak and rest in His grace?

Real Faithfulness

23 TRUST Walking

1. What do you like about this chapter?
2. What feelings, memories, or questions arise?
3. Have you ever tried the trust exercise?
4. What "alliances" do you need to leave?
5. When did you last ask the Lord for help?
6. What idols do you need His help to kick out?
7. In what do you not yet trust the Lord?
8. Where are you at on the Isaiah 30 continuum?

24 GO DEEPER

1. What do you like about this chapter?
2. What feelings, memories, or questions arise?
3. How has the Lord been testing you lately?
4. How has He been helping you pass the test?
5. Are your roots deeper than they were ten years ago? Why?
6. How has He proven His faithfulness to you?
7. Who is struggling and needs your prayer and help?
8. For what do you need prayer and help?

25 20/20/20

1. What do you like about this chapter?
2. What feelings, memories, or questions arise?
3. Do you like or dislike being still?
4. Try this for one month. Ask friends to pray for you.

REAL GENTLENESS

26 GOING LOW

1. What do you like about this chapter?
2. What feelings, memories, or questions arise?
3. What's the funniest thing you ever saw a child do?
4. How does it feel to see Jesus at your feet?
5. Are you ready to serve at others' feet?
6. When has He helped you know He understands?
7. Try some prayer conversation looking "down!"
8. Who needs you to truly serve them right now?

27 Even When We Disagree

1. What do you like about this chapter?
2. What feelings, memories, or questions arise?
3. What's the silliest spat you ever had?
4. What insecurities do you need to leave behind?
5. How much do you tune in to quarrelsome media?
6. Do you do more affirming or more criticizing?
7. Do you plan your week, your life with the Lord?
8. Is He following you, or are you following Him?

28 The Real Deal

1. What do you like about this chapter?
2. What feelings, memories, or questions arise?
3. What was your favorite food at grandma's house?
4. What is real humility?
5. Do you want all the fruit and gifts? Ask!
6. How does the Lord help you be more humble?
7. What miracles have you seen?
8. What miracles are you praying for?

Real Self-control

29 Doctor's Orders

1. What do you like about this chapter?
2. What feelings, memories, or questions arise?
3. What was your childhood neighborhood like?
4. How have you gained His wisdom the hard way?
5. How does He guide you through Scripture?
6. How does He guide you through wise counsel?
7. How does He guide you through prayer?
8. How does He guide you through inner witness?

30 Listen To Your Beloved

1. What do you like about this chapter?
2. What feelings, memories, or questions arise?
3. What is your funniest car travel story?
4. What is the enemy of self-control?
5. What are the two voices in every Christian?
6. How does the Lord communicate with you?
7. How does He let you know you're straying?

31 Stir It Up

1. What do you like about this chapter?
2. What feelings, memories, or questions arise?
3. What was one of your most fun vacations?
4. How are you defeating lust, greed, and pride?
5. How are you letting the Lord and others help you?
6. How are you helping others find victory?
7. How is a small group helping you in His mission?

The Adventure Ahead

32 A Wonderful Adventure

1. What do you like about this chapter?
2. What feelings, memories, or questions arise?
3. Do you have a favorite poet or songwriter?
4. How has the Lord helped you at past crossroads?
5. Is He offering a "road less traveled" right now?
6. What are His torches on the right path?
7. How much time do you savor His good stuff?
8. How much time do you taste the rotten stuff?
9. Do you truly want good fruit and the right path?

33 Destination Jesus

1. What do you like about this chapter?
2. What feelings, memories, or questions arise?
3. What delightful children do you know?
4. Do like wandering along another's agenda?
5. Are you willing or reluctant to follow Jesus?
6. What's the hardest task you have done for Jesus?
7. What bad storm of life did He get you through?
8. Who near you is in a bad storm of life now?
9. What does He want you to do for them?

34 Wellsprings, Buckets, and Seeds

1. What do you like about this chapter?
2. What feelings, memories, or questions arise?
3. What do you see with the Lord?
4. What changes will you make in the days ahead?

About the Author & Come Rest Ministries

Richard Speight, and his wife Kim, have been joyfully married for thirty-one years. They enjoy a simple life of prayer, witness, counsel, family, friendships, writing, drawing, hospitality, nature walks, and travel.

Dick and Kim founded Come Rest in 2006 after twenty-seven fruitful years of leading United Methodist churches. The mission of Come Rest Ministries is to help people rest in Jesus and bear His real fruit. Dick and Kim are known for their passion for Jesus and the lost, healing prayer, wisdom to help people discern the Lord's leading, ability to equip people to minister, and ministry to pastors and their families. Dick is an inspiring preacher and Kim a wise teacher, both sharing the gospel in simple ways. They can come to your church or city for retreats, awakenings, conferences, Sunday mornings, outreaches, or to consult with ministry leaders. They can customize a retreat for you or show you how the Come Rest small group model can bring real fruit to your neighborhood, church, or city.

The Come Rest ministry base is in Cedar Rapids, Iowa at the Speight's cozy home named "Rehoboth." At Rehoboth they lead personal retreats, Isaiah 58 outreach groups, and Wellsprings men's and women's accountability prayer groups. Come Rest also leads deeply moving Awakening of Love worship gatherings for people to rest secure and shine forth in Jesus' love.

A growing number of Christians are partnering with Come Rest Ministries. We invite you to explore how the Lord may be calling you to partner with us..

You may follow us at RichardFSpeight@ Twitter; Richard F. Speight Jr.@ Facebook; or our blog at www.comerest.blogspot.com.

For scheduling or more information, contact us at: www.comerestministries.com or kimspeight@comerestministries.com or 319-213-5684 or Come Rest Ministries, P.O. Box 11010, Cedar Rapids, Iowa 52410-1010

Recommendations for *Come Rest*

"I have known pastor Dick Speight for almost ten years. Besides being a close friend, I have known Dick to be a man of integrity. He's a man who lives out the role of a servant and finds delight and power in walking humbly with the Lord. Over the years, I've seen the Holy Spirit bless Dick with a growing and successful church and I've also watched, and stood with him, when the Holy Spirit tested him during trials. In all things, I have found Dick to be a man who steadfastly placed his trust in God. The lessons he shares in Come Rest are living realities, truths that he has personally experienced. His prescription for life's stresses has found their first fulfillment in Dick himself. Dick's soul rests in the goodness of the Almighty. Like the swallow, Dick too has made his nest at God's altar (Ps. 84:3). From his dwelling place in God's presence, Dick urges the reader, 'Come rest in the love of God.'"

Francis FrangipaneAuthor and Pastor

"'Work hard, play hard' is the mantra of a generation hopelessly striving to outrun our fear, anxiety and pain—and we are EXHAUSTED! Come Rest is not a 'stop and smell the roses' message, but rather insights into the real, freeing truth that finally gets us to where we've wanted and needed to go all along."

Glenn Shields
CEO, 21st Century Strategic Forums, St. Louis, Missouri

"Until the message of Come Rest was deeply in my spirit, I found myself constantly striving to love others and win the lost out of my insecurities. Learning to first rest in the Father's love as my position of strength for everything else I do has radically altered my family life, ministry and destiny!"

Caleb Plumb
Pastor, Encounter Christian Church; Director, Father's Heart International Cedar Rapids, Iowa

"This highly inspirational book gives credible witness to the author's call and lived experience of resting in Jesus. The reader comes away deeply motivated to let Jesus love us and lead us in this quest to rest in him."

Sister Nancy Hoffman FSPA
Prairiewoods Spirituality/Ecology Center, Cedar Rapids, Iowa

"Richard Speight has detailed a biblical remedy for a chronic condition in the body of Christ. Epidemic levels of unbridled busyness have overtaken the spiritual rest of many people of God. Without the intervention of a call to rest such as this, we may find ourselves rich in schedules and programs but with our hearts in a desert of turmoil. We must take the medicine now, allow the peace of the Lord to renew our minds, and emerge deeply at rest in HIM."

Ric Lumbard, Wind and Fire Ministries, Marion, Iowa

"With such unrest in our world, Jesus' great invitation of 'Come Rest' is truly a crucial message for this hour. In following a portion of Dick's agonizing journey in writing this book, I am not surprised at the depth, clarity, practicality, and simplicity of this work—because he trusted Jesus. His message is changing my life."

Steve Russell
Faith Outreach Ministries and Central Iowa Youth for Christ

"Dick Speight has a vital message for the churches of our time. Too often we think it's up to our efforts to make ourselves into effective disciples of Jesus and that we need the "right model" to make our church relevant. This book is a grace-filled call to fall deeply in love with Jesus, to spend time with Him, to be molded as humble followers of the One who does the work of transformation. In a distinctly prophetic spirit reminiscent of St. Francis and John Wesley, Richard makes it clear that when we rest in God's love, we become vessels of the Holy Spirit who remakes the world through our lives. This is all God's doing, not ours. The genius of this remarkable book is that when we allow our souls to stop striving and begin resting in God's love, then and only then is the power of God unleashed in the world to overcome social injustice and bring the transforming work of God to families in conflict, the oppressed, nations in chaos, and the poor."

Pastor Will Jackson
Presbyterian Missionary

"We live in a 24/7, non-stop, always connected, relentlessly busy world that leaves us more empty and alone than when we found it. Only God has a remedy for us. God has made Richard a rich blend of a desert father, an evangelical, contemplative, and a loving pastor. The result is a message that provokes you from all sides to rest in Jesus. 'Come Rest' is more than a book; it's an invitation into the life of rest you were designed to live."

Travis Kolder
Church Planter, Cedar Rapids House Church Network

Come Rest & Bear Real Fruit

with these Come Rest Ministries Audio Resources

On each of these CD's, short reflections, and teachings are accompanied by instrumental music to guide you in your "quest for rest." They can be used for devotional times, Bible studies, or church services. Listen to the whole CD at once, or enjoy the reflections one at a time.

Come Rest Meditations

Includes meditations on Jesus'invitation to rest, relieving burdens, forgiveness, identity, and more.

Reflections on His Real Love

Contains meditations on Grace, the leadership of the Lord in our lives, the discipline of contemplation, how to remain steady in the midst of times of shaking, and more.

To order one or both of these CDs, please send your name and address, a note describing your order, and your payment

($10 for one or $15 for both CDs, including shipping and handling) to:

Come Rest Ministries
P.O. Box 110
Cedar Rapids, IA 52410-1010

New books, DVD's, CD's and other media from Richard Speight are on the way. Keep current with us at www.comerestministries.com

"Resting in Jesus' love is for every moment. Resting in Him is the most fruitful thing you can do. As you rest in His love, His presence comes to rest on you, and His kingdom advances wherever you go!" - Dick Speight

Do you need a speaker?

Do you want Richard F. Speight, Jr. to speak to your group or event? Then contact Larry Davis at: **(623) 337-8710** or email: **ldavis@intermediapr.com** or use the contact form at: **www.intermediapr.com**.

Whether you want to purchase bulk copies of *Real Fruit: Receiving and Giving Jesus' Real Love* or buy another book for a friend, get it now at: **www.imprbooks.com**.

If you have a book that you would like to publish, contact Larry Davis, Publisher, at Intermedia Publishing Group, (623) 337-8710 or email: **ldavis@intermediapr.com** or use the contact form at: www.intermediapub.com.